JONATHAN'S RAINBOW

E. J. BENNER

SUNBURY PRESS

Mechanicsburg, PA USA

Published by Sunbury Press, Inc.
Mechanicsburg, Pennsylvania

www.sunburypress.com

For information about special discounts for bulk purchases, please contact Sunbury Press Orders Dept. at (855) 338-8359 or orders@sunburypress.com.

To request one of our authors for speaking engagements or book signings, please contact Sunbury Press Publicity Dept. at publicity@sunburypress.com.

ISBN: 978-1-62006-075-9 (Trade paperback)

Library of Congress Control Number: 2018958907

FIRST SUNBURY PRESS EDITION: September 2018

Product of the United States of America
0 1 1 2 3 5 8 13 21 34 55

Set in Bookman Old Style
Designed by Crystal Devine
Cover by Terry Kennedy
Edited by Lawrence Knorr

Continue the Enlightenment!

Dedicated to

*Miranda and Raya, the best sissies
a guy could ever hope for!*

Clay, the big brother that he idolizes

CONTENTS

ACKNOWLEDGMENTS

Miranda, Raya, and Jonathan – "All my lovin'!"

Mom, Dad, Family and Friends – Thank you for your support and encouragement.

Sharon Herr – Thank you for your editing and support (mental and spiritual).

Debbie (my computer genius) – Thank you for putting up with all my endless questions and computer issues.

Lydia (my tech) – Thank you niece/daughter!

Sharon Ailes – Thank you for all the little notebooks to encourage me to always be writing.

Cathy and Pam – See . . . my constant reading finally paid off.

Writers Club (Ed and Kathleen) – I brought so little to the table and took away so much. Thank you from the bottom of my heart.

Pat Lorenz – Your support and thoughtfulness helped me through the early years. Your journal is a treasure.

Miranda and Clay – Thank you for all that you do: editing, telling tales, PR and for always having my back. I couldn't manage without you.

INTRODUCTION

Dear Reader,

I am a single mother of three children. My oldest daughter, Miranda, is my mini-me. Raya, the second, is adopted from China, and Jonathan, my youngest child, has special needs. I am a product of divorced parents . . . a middle child . . . and divorced myself.

I have wanted to write a book for as long as I can remember. I have so much subject matter to choose from . . . literally in my backyard.

Jonathan's story needed to be told and I needed to tell it. I wanted to share with everyone the amazing young man he has become and the path that led us here. It wasn't always easy, in fact, the path was very rocky with many twists, turns, and even a few forks in the road, but nonetheless, so many people have helped to shape our lives and I am grateful.

My life has been littered with mistakes but I'm optimistic that these were strategically placed lessons that my family and I can learn from. What's a good life without a little bit of excitement, anyway? I have made mistakes over the years. Hopefully, I have learned from my mistakes, without causing too much damage.

I am an emotional collector of items, causing me to collect snippets of our lives, over the years—written on used envelopes, napkins—anything that I had available at the time all in the hope to capture the thought or memory before it slipped away, like so many things did when I was so busy with young children. These scraps of info were stuck in a folder or various notebooks. They weren't always in the same place. I thought I had plenty of time to organize these memories. But, we all know how quickly time slips away and before we know it, years have gone by.

Some paper scraps of our memories were lost in the throes of several moves. Some are still being found at an unexpected moment while cleaning out a forgotten box—a box shoved under the bed or lost under mountains of other boxes in a storage closet.

It's like Christmas morning, opening gifts when I find a long-lost scrap of paper with some wonderful tale written on it. A memory that might have been forgotten, laying in a box with other treasures from the past. It will never cease to amaze me how letters arranged on a page can bring about a vivid recollection of a wonderful memory, a funny moment, or a lesson waiting to be remembered and learned.

I am always writing things down in little notebooks that I carry around in my purse or in the console of the car. Inspiration comes to me while driving . . . in between Jonathan's iPad chattering and his constant changing of the radio stations. Sometimes, I block out everything and dream of being published. For as long as my daughters remember, they recall me talking about this distant fantasy of writing a book, of being published, of sharing our stories, but most importantly of sharing Jonathan's impactful touch on our lives.

In this book writing process, my daughters have reminded me of things that have happened and wanted to add to the story. I never knew if when I answered the phone it would be one of my daughters laughing through a memory or more likely just calling to ask how long chicken can keep in the refrigerator—Mom life. My mother and friends have also added some anecdotes to the story.

Jonathan was born when not much was known about Down syndrome. I knew nothing! Thank goodness so much has changed. We have all learned so much. I am grateful for the massive influx of information now that new parents can be comforted instead of intimidated with medical jargon and threats of an uncertain future. However, a small part of me can't help but be bitter that these resources were not available to us—to Jonathan. I can't help but think that our unknown, oftentimes lonely, journey down our tumultuous path would have been easier with all the tour guides and markers now readily available. If only I had known *this* or heard about *that* therapy maybe he would be there, not here. Fortunately, for me, I have a wonderful, happy son and phenomenal support system that keeps these thoughts at bay. As Miranda used to say, "Now, if I have a choice whether Jonathan had Down syndrome or not, I honestly don't know if I would take it away. It's part of him and he's happy." While as a mother I can say that my choice would be different than hers, I can't say that I don't agree. It is a part of him and calling him happy is an understatement.

My apologies if I offend anyone. I feel like a lot of parents were much more organized and structured than I was. So many parents seemed to be so much more together than I was. It didn't help that I felt truly alone. Divorced, I handled countless appointments alone. The girls were too young and my mother was from a different generation. She didn't always understand the doctors' appointments, therapy sessions, or a constant fight for his opportunities.

This book is about my family's struggles, triumphs, and many heartwarming situations. I hope our day-to-day anecdotes will help someone in the same situation. I hope our stories will make someone laugh. That is my intention. If at the end of the day, just one person smiles because of this book, I can rest easy.

Our lives were a work in progress . . . many days I was flying from the seat of my pants. Some days, I couldn't find any clean pants. Jonathan has taught me so much.

Thank you, Jonathan. I am a much better person because of you.

The chapters are presented in a thematic way. Each chapter is designated for a specific topic. The individual chapters are in somewhat of a chronological order . . . from Jonathan's birth to present. The dated excerpts are taken from a journal that my friend Pat Lorenz wrote. These excerpts I have inserted where I deemed appropriate to the story. Pat started the journal the day Jonathan was born and gave it to me on his first birthday. For this, I am forever grateful.

So, this book is for all the Jonathans . . . past, present, and future. It's also for all the families of Jonathans, that have been changed forever. You are not alone. I hope I can serve as a lowly tour guide on your journey. May your path be smooth. This is our journey.

1: THE BEGINNING

There was a shuffle at the crib. The nurses were rushing over. I said, "What's wrong with my baby?" You could feel the tension and urgency in the room. I kept repeating, "What's wrong with my baby? What's going on?" The atmosphere in the room had changed from a normal delivery to an emergency. Dr. Wood said, "Everything is fine. Ladies, let's not get the mother excited. I am trying to stitch her up."

They whisked my newborn baby away. I had no idea what was going on. I knew I had a baby boy and a normal delivery but that was it. Something must have been terribly wrong.

Everything was a blur from that point forward. I remember being told that they were running some tests. We were told that our baby might have a heart problem. They were running tests for that possibility. We were told later that he might have Down syndrome. That test takes about a week to get the results.

It was May 7, 1998. I was determined to have a natural VBAC (Vaginal Birth after Cesarean). The pregnancy went well. I felt satisfied that I took pretty good care of myself during the pregnancy and followed the rules. I didn't even drink coffee, which was a sacrifice for me.

I was 37 when Jonathan was born. I tried so hard to get pregnant. I had taken fertility drugs and given myself shots at that certain time of the month. I cried every month when I got my period. My friends would get pregnant and I would be happy for them but so sad for the baby that I wanted so desperately.

When I started seeing double and triple, which is a side effect of the fertility medicine, I decided to give it a break. We decided to consider adoption. We went through with all the tedious paperwork,

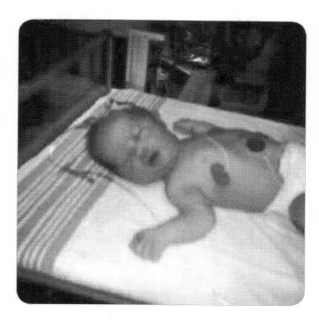

and we played the waiting game. The adoption agency promised a nine-month wait but it turned into one and a half years. During this time, I became pregnant with Jonathan.

People would tell me to relax, and I would get pregnant. That was so maddening. I wasn't sure when I was supposed to relax before, during, or after having intercourse! Well . . . another cliché is that when you adopt and get pregnant, it's because you stop worrying about it. I liked to think that we were doubly blessed!

We were so excited to become pregnant. I opted not to have the prenatal amniocentesis done. When an expectant mother is over age 35, the likelihood of giving birth to a child with Down syndrome (among other things) increases. I discussed it with my doctor. He asked what we would do if the fetus tested positive for birth defects.

Abortion was not an option. I felt that we tried too hard to get pregnant. It probably would have been better to know before the birth, but in hindsight, I wouldn't have changed my mind. Knowing me, all that an early diagnosis would have done was cause worry during pregnancy. I am glad I made that decision, but the unexpected delivery of a baby with Down syndrome was devastating. I can honestly say it was a huge shock that took a little while for me to accept. Our friends and family were waiting for us to call and give them the good news about the birth of our child. We didn't want to talk to anybody. It was as if talking about it would make it become a reality. We even unplugged the phone in our hospital room, so that no one could call us.

I felt numb from my head to my toes and my brain felt fuzzy. I was living in a fog. We were waiting to hear from the doctor about what was going on with our baby. I remember being impatient to hear something but not wanting to know at the same time. My mind was racing with "what ifs" and "whys." Jonathan was in the Neonatal Intensive Care Unit (NICU) for 19 days. They ran a lot of tests and ruled out heart problems. Thank goodness! He had trouble with oxygen exchange and had to be fed through a little tube. He had a floppy epiglottis which contributed to the poor oxygen exchange. I can remember looking at him in his little incubator crib. He had tubes and wires everywhere. I couldn't look at him at first, but when I did, I cried and cried. I kept thinking, "Why me?" That may sound terrible but I am being honest and feel comfortable sharing this now because he is one of the best things that ever happened to me.

Then, when I could look at him, I cried because he was so tiny, so vulnerable with all those tubes and wires all over him. He seemed to be strong . . . a fighter right from the start. I looked around the NICU, at babies much tinier than Jonathan and felt so much gratitude. Some babies didn't seem to have family members to cuddle them. Jonathan was a lucky little guy. He was blessed with family and friends to be checking on him all the time.

Jonathan's first visitors were my mom, my dad, and step-mom, Miranda, my sister Cindy, my brother Bryon, my Lock Haven friends, my church friends, my work friends, my high school friends and, of course, the pastor. We were truly blessed. Forever etched in my memories were some of the reactions and concerns I received from everyone.

One thing I want to accomplish by writing this book is to become an advocate for mothers of newborns with Down syndrome. I tell them that whatever they are feeling is normal. No one expects to have a child with special needs. The future seems so unknown and scary. I would love to shake the mothers' hands and say, "Congratulations. You are in for the ride of your life. It will be like a roller coaster with lots of ups and downs, but the ride is so worth it. Be prepared to be frustrated, overwhelmed, humbled, stressed, and loved beyond measure." Raising any child, typically-developing or otherwise, comes with its own set of challenges. Jonathan was different from his sisters just as any child is different from their siblings.

May 8, 1998

This story begins yesterday . . . your birthday. I talked to your mommy five hours after your birth. I cried. She cried for a tiny new person with a weak heart. I prayed that God would not take you from her. I prayed for her strength and courage as she waited for tests, doctor's reports, and updates on your condition. We spoke of Down syndrome . . . a condition that would make you different than other children. I tried to hope that it was a mistake, but as I talked with God I felt comforted. My prayers were that Jonathan Banks Kellenberger would prove to have a healthy heart . . . that you would be a part of our lives and that with or without Down syndrome, you would be given the opportunity to bless many lives. We will all be blessed by you.

Today, I got the chance to meet you. The neonatal intensive care unit housed many babies . . . all so small and weak. But in a corner, there was a 7-pound beautiful baby boy. I spoke your name and you struggled to open your eyes. I was lost in the moment. I put my finger in your hand and you closed your tiny fingers around it. You struggled to remove tubes and I saw, not a baby with Down syndrome, but a wonderful, responsive little baby who captured my heart.

Jonathan, we do not know what our lives will bring us, but I truly believe your parents have been given a special gift. I'm not sure why I feel this way. I simply know that meeting you, touching you, and seeing you open your eyes gave me a comfort. A peace that God has something extraordinary in store for us all.

The hours and days that followed were a big blur. A candy striper (do they even call them that anymore?) came in the room to see if I needed anything. She asked if we decided what we were going to do. I said, "What are you talking about?" Apparently, we could have opted to give him up for adoption. As shocked and scared as we were, the thought of giving up our precious baby never crossed our minds. We banned her from the room.

The first-night stay in the hospital was awful. Everyone had gone home, and I was left to a sleepless night alone. I felt like I was on an emotional roller coaster. I was wrung out and exhausted to the core—physically and mentally. I laid in bed, tears streaming down my face. I wanted someone to hold me and tell me everything would be ok. But I laid there all alone, silently crying, my tears making my starchy pillow damp.

The nurses would tiptoe in and do what they had to do, then disappear again. I felt like there was a sign on the outside of my door, "crazy woman inside . . . enter with extreme caution." That was okay. I didn't want to talk to anyone.

The room was dark, the TV was on, but I couldn't concentrate on the program. I was staring at the screen, but my mind was racing in a million different directions. I didn't know what to think or feel. I was so afraid of what the future held. I was afraid I couldn't do what I needed to do for this little guy. I kept thinking "Why God? Why? Why me? I have no idea what I am doing. Will I be able to love this little person? Will I be able to take care of him?"

It was soon time for me to leave the hospital and Jonathan had to stay in the NICU. They wanted to make sure everything was okay because he was having trouble with his oxygen exchange. That was the worst feeling . . . leaving my baby in the hospital. I knew he was in good hands and he would get the best of care. I have undying gratitude and admiration for the nurses in the NICU at Harrisburg Hospital. They kept assuring me that he would be fine, but it was still one of the hardest things I've ever had to do.

I remember driving home, looking all around me, but not really seeing anything. I remember thinking that everything looked the same as when I went to the hospital to deliver a baby. The trees were still green. People were still out and about, involved in their daily routines. How could my surroundings still look the same when my whole world had changed so drastically?

> *May 9, 1998*
> It feels like a storm has erupted. After a storm, we can
> look for a rainbow. You, our sweet special child, may be that
> rainbow. You will brighten and enlighten our future.
>
> Today, I pray God will continue to help you improve. I pray
> God will give your Mommy, Daddy, and Miranda comfort as
> they come home and resume everyday life. I pray that soon the
> storm will calm and a rainbow will appear.

We got the diagnosis of Down syndrome about a week after he was born. We were certain of this before, but getting the lab results back made it official. My sister was reassuring me that there were worse disorders. She said kids with Down syndrome are lovable.

I couldn't think too far in the future. I was struggling with the present. She said that she had spoken to someone that worked with children with special needs. They said that kids with Down syndrome like order and routine. We had a good laugh. I was pretty laid back and not orderly at all! Oh my, how my life has changed!

Jonathan's breathing became more difficult. They had to put him on a respirator. A doctor with a bow tie and no bedside manner very bluntly told me that he would probably need a tracheotomy. This was beyond upsetting to me. I told myself that was not going to happen. I prayed and prayed that he would not need a trach. I discussed with the nurses other options for facilities if the worst happened and he did need the tracheotomy procedure. Dr. Bowtie was not going to touch my son. It felt good to get my energy directed in a positive way, something that I might have had a little control over since my life seemed so out of control.

I laid my hands on Jonathan and prayed. Our pastor, a sweet man, came to the hospital and prayed with Jonathan and me. I was very determined that he was not going to have a trach. Our prayers were answered. His breathing improved and he was soon able to breathe on his own. I didn't realize it at the time, but we had a faith healing. The miracle of prayers never cease to amaze me.

May 15, 1998

Oh, Jonathan, you are so little in that big, bright room. Noise is all around you. They bend your feet in ways that make you uncomfortable. The tubes, machines, etc. which constantly monitor your condition are so foreign to a new baby. I pray God gives you comfort until you can join a gentler atmosphere . . . home.

Your mom and I took a break and had some lunch. Upon our return to the unit, we were asked to leave. Your breathing became more difficult for you and they put you on a respirator. We returned to find (again) a large tube down your throat and we cried. Your mom held you. We cried for your struggle. Sweet, sweet baby Jonathan, I pray you feel the sunshine soon.

During all the breathing situation, the doctor told your mommy you have Down syndrome. Jonathan, I saw her go from a very high point this morning to defeat by midafternoon. I know a part of her and everyone who shares their lives was hoping for a miracle . . . a mistaken diagnosis. We wanted you from the beginning but oh the changes, adjustments, etc. they will make as they refocus on an unfamiliar way of looking at parenting.

This news hit hard. You will be different than a "normal" child. You will require many months and years of physical therapy. Your mental capabilities are unknown now but will require special attention. Your physical appearance may be a bit different. All so new to me and many who share your life. Many days may be tough but many days will bring a special love and joy to your parents. I truly believe they will be blessed by you and I will be a part of it.

May we all learn to appreciate the good things in life and to never take for granted the God-given gifts we have!

Jonathan's NICU stay was only 19 days, which doesn't seem that long, in retrospect. At the time, it was very traumatic. I wanted to keep things as normal as possible for Miranda. She was in kindergarten at the time. We got into a routine. I would visit Jonathan at the hospital while Miranda was at school. Usually, a friend would get her after school until I got home. Then we would drive back down to see Jonathan in the evening. This was an hour's drive. Everything took timing and planning.

We would take Miranda along. She loved seeing her little brother. She wasn't allowed to hold him at first and she couldn't wait to hold the little guy. We learned to properly scrub our hands. Miranda took these instructions very personally. For years, her hands would crack and bleed every single winter due to vigorous scrubbing. She had her hands scrubbed raw, poor thing.

I wanted desperately to breastfeed Jonathan, but he had a feeding tube. I would use an electric pump and store the breast milk. The nurses used it to feed him. It wasn't always convenient, but it worked.

My sister advised me to get a pacifier for him. Since he wasn't sucking naturally on a bottle or breast, he needed that type of stimulation. We tried that, but he wasn't always very interested. The things I took for granted with Miranda . . . things that happened naturally . . . like the sucking instinct, it was a whole new world. I had so much to learn.

The last night of Jonathan's hospital stay was in a regular room on the pediatric floor. I stayed with him. I wanted to make sure I could handle anything that happened. He still had the monitor on that measured his oxygen exchange. A machine would go off and beep like crazy if it went below a certain amount. It also went off if the device came off his toe. It beeped a lot that night. We didn't get much sleep and I was petrified to go home with him. They assured me that everything would be fine. He didn't need a heart monitor at home. I am sure I asked this question a million times!

It was so nice to have him home, but I worried about him. I remember thinking, if there was a test given to see if a parent was competent to take home and care for their baby, I would not have passed. I couldn't believe the nurses at the hospital felt I was prepared for what was ahead.

He slept in a little cradle beside my bed. I kept waking up to see if he was still breathing. We still joke about me always holding a mirror under his nose so that I could see the condensation of his breath. He was a great sleeper. In fact, he slept so well that I had to wake him up to feed him during the night. The pediatrician wanted me to feed him every two hours because he wasn't gaining weight. This feeding schedule was really a struggle because he wanted to sleep instead of eating.

When we left the hospital, we were in the care of our pediatrician and the orthopedic doctor for his club feet. Jonathan passed all the cardiology tests, so we were cleared there. He had to have an eye exam and hearing test after we left the hospital. He cleared these tests also.

2: STATISTICS

Down syndrome, or trisomy 21, happens because of extra genetic material in the 21st pair of chromosomes. This extra chromosomal material alters the course of development and causes the characteristics associated with Down syndrome. It's hard to believe that this tiny bit of extra matter in the chromosomal makeup can affect someone so greatly.

In the United States, one in every 691 births is born with Down syndrome. The chances increase as the maternal age increases. After the age of 35, the ratio is one in 350 births. At age 40, the mother has a one in 100 chance. At age 45, the incidence jumps up to a one in thirty chance of giving birth to a baby with Down syndrome.

Down syndrome is not racist or for the poor only. It occurs in all races and socioeconomic levels.

There are three types of Down syndrome:

1. Trisomy 21 (nondisjunction) – this type makes up 95% of the cases

2. Translocation – this is four percent and is the only type that has hereditary components

3. Mosaic – this includes only one percent of all Down syndrome cases

There are prenatal tests that can diagnose many birth defects. Amniocentesis and blood work are common ones used, especially when the expectant mother is 35 years of age and older. With amniocentesis, there is a small chance of miscarriage. I tried so hard

Jonathan being cute.

to get pregnant, I wasn't willing to take this chance. I discussed the situation with my doctor. He asked me what I would do if the tests came back positive. I said, "Nothing."

With that, he replied, "then don't have the additional testing done."

I am so glad that I didn't. It would have really caused me to stress and worry unnecessarily.

The test they typically perform after birth is called karyotyping. With a blood sample, they match up the chromosomal arrangement with a "normal" one. I can remember waiting for this test to come back from the lab. It took about a week to confirm the diagnosis. We were pretty sure by that point of his diagnosis, but it was still an agonizing wait.

The physical traits most commonly associated with Down syndrome are low muscle tone, small stature, an upward slant to the eyes, and a single crease across the center of the palm of the hand. They may possess characteristics to different degrees or not at all.

All Down syndrome children experience cognitive (intellectual) delays. These can vary from mild to moderate. Each child is an individual and should not be stereotyped.

Thank goodness, the life expectancy has increased dramatically. In 1983 the life expectancy was 25 years. Today, the life expectancy is 60. This, of course, varies depending on the individual's health issues.

Some health risks that are increased in Down syndrome individuals are congenital heart defects, respiratory issues, hearing problems, Alzheimer's disease, childhood leukemia, and thyroid problems. Just being aware of these issues can help you be proactive and diagnose conditions early. Early diagnosis of these otherwise life-threatening health conditions is instrumental in continuing to increase life expectancy among those with Down syndrome.

> *May 27, 1998*
>
> Already you have made many people appreciate the people in our lives and the things that we have. You will remind us to not take for granted the many blessings we are given. You are our "rainbow," Jonathan. Continue to brighten and enlighten our lives . . .
>
> I rubbed your face against mine and it brought relief. You are the miracle we prayed for . . . a gift from God!

3: SIBLINGS

As a parent of three children, I worried a lot about giving everyone enough attention and meeting their needs successfully. Add a child with special needs to the mix and I was completely overwhelmed. I was outnumbered and steamrolled on many occasions.

When Jonathan was born and in the NICU, we were also in the process of adopting Raya. I was concerned about how to handle two babies. The NICU nurse said it would be good stimulation and good for both. He said that Jonathan would follow Raya's every move. Boy, was he right. Raya has been stimulation for the whole

Miranda and Clay's wedding, September 3, 2016.

family from the moment she got off the plane! The family dynamics of having a child with special needs is amazing.

From Jonathan's birth until he was two years old, he had many, many appointments. Therapists would come to the house, which was helpful, but very overwhelming. Some weeks we had ten or eleven appointments.

I think those first two years were a blur. I remember thinking that someone else had taken over my body, and I had lost all control of my life! My saving grace was when friends and family would come and play with Miranda and Raya or take them somewhere. A lot of times they would be naughty to get my attention when I was talking to a therapist or caregiver.

I know I prayed a lot. I prayed that God would give me the strength to handle all daily situations and give all my children the attention they needed. I was operating on a day-to-day basis!

> *August 28, 1998*
>
> Eve,
>
> Your time with the children is so, so short. You get down and fell overwhelmed. You nearly cry as you tell me you feel guilty if you do not have time with Jonathan to do his exercises. I feel for you.
>
> Keep the faith. My prayers are for you each day.

Jonathan adores his sisters, and he loves them unconditionally. He even forgave them when they decided to do their own physical therapy on him. The physical therapist was working with Jonathan on our treadmill. He was probably two years old. He didn't walk independently until he was two and a half. The girls watched the therapist work with him using the treadmill and when she left, they decided they were his personal therapists.

They tried to get him to walk on the treadmill, and he got pushed off but caught under the conveyor belt, and it spun. He still has the scar from that. Their careers as his therapists were quickly over. They did therapy with him without even trying. They didn't need a treadmill. He always wanted to keep up with them and do what they were doing. That was the best therapy!

Jonathan was approximately five years old when we discovered he had Celiac disease. There was little known about this disease at that time. When we would meet someone new, Raya would introduce her little brother and say he has Celiac disease; she didn't mention

Down syndrome. It was so funny. In her eyes, that was his big issue, the Celiac disease, which it did completely alter his diet and meal times.

Up until that point, Cheerios were his favorite food and they also served a therapeutic purpose of improving his fine motor coordination. When he had to give up Cheerios, they weren't making a gluten-free alternative yet. The gluten-free foods were limited and not the tastiest. His sisters still bring up the first gluten-free brownie we made—they thought the main ingredient was sand! Once gluten-free diets became more popular, more options were available to Jonathan. The day we gave him his first gluten-free pretzel, he held it in his hands and took small bites out of a single pretzel. After each bite he would spin around the kitchen, clutching the remaining pretzel piece to his chest, moaning with delight.

Recently, I gave Jonathan a gluten-free donut. They were frozen, needing to be heated in the microwave. He refused to eat it. He didn't think it was gluten free! Of course, it was probably awful. Who wants to eat a donut that has been frozen?

When Miranda was a teenager, we had some trying times, as most moms and teenage daughters do. One time, all four of us were walking in the mall. Miranda and I were arguing. I can't even remember what it was about. Jonathan was in between us, holding our hands. Before we realized what he was doing, he pushed our hands together and let go, forcing us to hold hands with each other. It was a sign to call a truce. Jonathan has no room for negativity in his rose-colored world!

Vacations were and still are always interesting. We usually go to the beach for a few days or a week. The rest of us are ready to rest and relax. Jonathan's body does not know rest and relaxation. If we are lucky, he might sleep in until 7:00. Then, on many occasions, he ends up at my bedside, my glasses and slippers in his hands saying, "me eat." His stomach dictates our schedule. Jonathan loves to eat! Now, that he has a computer, he can entertain himself for a while before he demands attention and food!

We love the beach in Chincoteague, Virginia and Virginia Beach, but we love anywhere we go if we are all together. We've been hiking at Rickett's Glen and had a Disney vacation.

One highlight about vacation was Raya getting all dressed up and taking Jonathan out for ice cream. They were probably fourteen and fifteen that year. We usually dress up one night and go out to eat. Jonathan loves getting dressed up, especially if it involves a tie. Raya decided to have a special night with Jonathan by taking him out, just the two of them. Miranda said the best part of her vacation was seeing the look on his face when he is having fun. He thoroughly enjoys the beach and the swimming in the ocean.

I don't go out very far in the ocean. I don't like to ride the waves. I love the beach, but not being in the water. Clay (Miranda's husband), Miranda, and Raya will take Jonathan out and ride the waves. Jonathan has always loved the water. When he was young (one and a half years old) and couldn't walk yet, he would army crawl from under our beach umbrella toward the crashing waves. He looked like a baby sea turtle. Prior to him learning to swim, he always had to wear a floatie while near a pool. His was like a wetsuit with foam padding to ensure floating. He didn't understand that he needed it to swim safely and there were a few occasions where he would attempt jumping off our diving board without it! Thankfully, now he's a better swimmer than most of the family. He participates in the Special Olympics swimming. His sisters discovered that he was a more skilled swimmer than we realized when they were all swimming in the pool one day. Jonathan swam out to the middle of the deep end and would say "Help, help me!". Of course, each time he did this, his sisters would swim to his rescue. He would then dunk them and swim happily away!

One year, I rented paddle boards. They made sure that Jonathan got up and held on to him, so he wouldn't fall. Jonathan would sit cross-legged on the front of the board and dive into waves as they came crashing toward the board.

We have so much fun when we are all together. In fact, Jonathan and I won't go to the beach if Clay, Miranda, and Raya can't go. It's just not as much fun. Besides, Miranda usually takes Jonathan to the beach one of the mornings of our vacation, so I can sleep in.

We have had so many challenging times. He used to run away. Everywhere we went, we had to keep eyes on him constantly. We had special locks on the door so he wouldn't escape. His weakness was always elevators. He loved them. Once at the beach, when Jonathan was about eight years old, he ran out of our hotel room and into an elevator. We began frantically searching for him once we realized he wasn't in the room with us. Thankfully, we found him downstairs. He didn't realize what he had done was wrong.

We also had a dog, Claude, that liked to run around the neighborhood. One day, the dog got out of the backyard. Jonathan must have decided to chase him. I didn't realize that Jonathan was

Jonathan finding shells on the beach, September 2017.

missing for a few minutes. Then, I was frantic. I started searching the neighborhood with the help of friends. I saw a police car parked along the street. I thought I would ask him if he saw Jonathan, hoping he could help me. I pulled alongside the police car to speak to the officer and saw Jonathan sitting in the back seat. I was so relieved, I didn't know if I should laugh or cry. The worst part was Jonathan's attire. He was wearing Raya's flowered rain boots, boxer shorts, and a t-shirt. That's it. I'm sure the police officer had a story to tell about the incident when he got back to the precinct.

At that point, he was very much about instant gratification. If he wanted to ride the elevator or run after the dog, he was going to do it that very second. This slowly transitioned into at least telling us (or trying to) that he was going to run off somewhere. Now we've finally transitioned into him asking first. This has saved me lots of stress and unwanted police presence.

One evening, when Raya and Jonathan were fourteen and fifteen, I was laying on the couch. I was exhausted—totally worn out. It's one of those parental moments where you hope your physical presence is enough parenting for the time being! The mind was shut down!

Raya and Jonathan were dancing beside me. They were loving life. Then, Raya decided to hurdle the coffee table. I was too tired to protest. Because she was such a great big sister, she showed Jonathan how to do it! A small part of my brain that was still functioning, rationalized that this was good physical therapy! He copies everything she does.

Jonathan gave it his best effort, but his little legs just couldn't get over the table. I put an end to the shenanigans after a couple of attempts. I decided we didn't need anything broken that night (furniture or bones)!

Miranda was always the nurturer. She was and still is mothering to Jonathan. In fact, she still goes to appointments with me. We try to make it work with her schedule. I value her input and always ask her opinion for most decisions regarding Jonathan's well-being.

One time they were at the swimming pool. Jonathan told her that someone was staring at him. Miranda told him it was because he is such a good swimmer. He happily accepted this as the reason and continued to have a fun day in the sun with his sister.

Miranda has a Master's degree in Occupational Therapy with a minor in sign language. In the summers, she worked for Easter Seals. She was a counselor at camps for those with special needs. I think her relationship with Jonathan had an impact on her career decisions.

Raya and Jonathan are only ten and a half months apart. Jonathan has always been tiny, so they look much further apart in age. For one and a half months each year, they are the same age.

I will never forget one time when they were both four. We stopped at a little store to get ice cream. Raya ordered for herself (she was always very independent), then said, "and my little brother will have a vanilla in a cone."

The clerk thought they were so cute and asked her age. She said, "I'm four."

The clerk then asked how old her little brother was and she of course very nonchalantly said, "four."

The clerk did a double take and looked back and forth between them. You know she was thinking that they couldn't be twins. For one, their size was very different. For another, Raya is Chinese! We really got a chuckle as we explained the situation to the poor lady.

Raya is more the "typical" sibling. She tells Jonathan to grow up and act his age! But, she also helps him make his bed and pick out his clothes so that he will look good. Before she left for college, she would help him get ready for bed if I was busy. She and her friends would babysit a lot for us.

One day, when Raya was in fifth grade, she approached me and said, "I wish I was a problem child too, like Miranda and Jonathan so, I could get some attention."

I said, "We will get you a dog." We went to the SPCA and picked out Claude Monet, the dog that liked to run away. He ran off every chance he could. The neighbors hated us, but Raya was happy.

I asked Raya what she thought were some pros and cons of being Jonathan's sister. She thought that he had opened her eyes to the special needs community. Raya felt that growing up with Jonathan made her kinder and more empathetic. She has had to be more understanding. Raya felt that living with Jonathan has taught her to help people who can't help themselves or need help reaching their goals. Raya attended culinary school. Her long-term goal is to work with people with special needs, either through cooking therapy or by owning a restaurant that employs mostly individuals with special needs. She felt that a downside to being Jonathan's sibling is knowing that he is our number one priority for the rest of our lives. We always must be concerned for him and his future. She knows that she and Miranda will be responsible for Jonathan when I am gone. Raya has grown into a very focused, driven young lady. I am proud of her and her accomplishments. She became responsible at a young age. Maybe I made her be too responsible before she needed to be. I know it has not always been easy for her, because of the two of them being so close in age. She has had to give up a lot and sometimes she had to give up some of her own activities to watch Jonathan.

Both girls would never date anyone that didn't get along with Jonathan. That was always a must . . . to see how boyfriends interacted with him. Miranda jokingly called it "The Jonathan Test". When she found someone, who passed with flying colors, she married him! I guess the test isn't too bad after all!

They both miss him horribly when they are away. We went to visit regularly when they were at college. They didn't care if I came to visit, but Jonathan can't get there without me! Once, I stayed in a hotel room and he stayed with his sister in her dorm room! A win-win situation for everyone! I could get some sleep and they had quality time.

When we first moved Miranda into college, Jonathan folded himself into her laundry basket so that he could stay. When her roommate came, he ushered her out the door because he thought that he was Miranda's roommate! When Raya left for college, it was lonely for us. It took a while for it to sink in that she was really gone. Jonathan would look in her bedroom expecting her to be in her bed!

Of course, all their friends have heard all about him and couldn't wait to meet him.

Miranda used to take Jonathan trick-or-treating on her college campus. All her friends were ready for him and had treats for him.

Miranda's husband, Clay, is the big brother Jonathan always hoped for. Clay and even his parents have special nicknames for Jonathan. I am so blessed.

Miranda and I took a knitting class on Thursday nights. While we were in class, Clay and Jonathan went shopping and out to eat. Clay would also work on Jonathan's speech and manners while they were sitting at the table. Have I mentioned how blessed I am?

Clay met Jonathan for the first time at Jonathan's fifteenth birthday party. We were having a basketball-themed party, and Clay brought a basketball for Jonathan's gift. He didn't even know about the theme. He had asked Miranda what Jonathan liked, and she said balls. Clay brought Jonathan the perfect gift and even better yet . . . played basketball with him. Clay knew he had to make a good first impression with Jonathan because Jonathan meant so much to Miranda.

Clay said that Jonathan was the first person with Down syndrome that he had been around. Communication was tough at first, but now they pick on each other all the time. Miranda must constantly tell them to behave. She tells Clay that she will put him on time out if he doesn't behave! Jonathan thinks this is so funny and will purposefully try to get him in trouble. Jonathan requests to sit beside Clay at family functions; he tells everyone where to sit when we go out to eat.

Jonathan was in Miranda and Clay's wedding. A few weeks before the wedding, Clay and some of the groomsmen took Jonathan out for a special "Jonathan friendly" bachelor party at the Texas

Roadhouse Steakhouse. They told the waitress that it was his birthday. When she brought the saddle out for Jonathan to sit on and started singing, he was confused because he knew it wasn't his birthday, but he gladly got on the saddle and Clay snapped a few pictures of the "birthday boy".

I recently asked Miranda what some pros and cons were of being a sibling of a child with special needs. She said she doesn't see him any differently than anyone else. She does think that she learned to be more patient and compassionate because of Jonathan.

Miranda always got a kick out of people thinking that he is her child when they are out in public. He looks a lot younger than he really is and acts a lot younger too. People give them weird looks sometimes.

She mentioned that he required a lot of my attention when she was growing up. I know that I depended on her a lot—too much. She missed many outings with her friends to watch over her little brother. I think I did okay, though. Miranda has grown into a lovely, caring person.

Both girls had to mature quicker and become responsible early in their lives. If there was something I could change, that would be it. I am sorry, girls. I used to tell them that we are in this life together and I was their biggest fan. Jonathan and I were at every sporting event, concert, banquet, and musical that they were involved in, but I deeply regret taking some of their teenage time from them.

Miranda and Clay recently bought a huge, old house. Every room needed repair work and paint. Jonathan had his own bedroom in their house. Do you want to guess what room got fixed up first? He wanted yellow paint on the walls, but Miranda didn't want all yellow walls! They compromised and painted three walls gray with an accent wall of yellow. He has gray carpet (of course, the first room to get carpet installed) and twin beds.

Every time we go to visit, Jonathan takes something to put in his room. On our last visit, it was a pillow. He brings things in plastic bags and discreetly leaves the items when we leave! Yay! Less stuff at my house!

Miranda always tells Jonathan how smart he is. She tells him he is handsome and kind. She tells him daily that she loves him and that he is the best brother ever. She left him this note on his bed the night before the first day of eleventh grade. I had strict instructions to read it to him as soon as he got home.

August 20, 2017

Jon K,

I'm so happy that I got to see you at Kari's shower yesterday. You were cracking me up with all your jokes. You're such a funny guy. I brought you two pins for your new backpack. One is the British flag. You can tell people that sissy went there and got it for you. The other is a frog. I know how much you like froggies and it will be your reminder to always wear your underwear. "FROGGIE, YOU FORGOT YOUR UNDERWEAR!" I hope you have the best day of school tomorrow. Get a good night's sleep and have good dreams about school. I bet everyone is excited to see you and hear about your summer.

Remember, use your iPad for class, not games or pictures. Listen with your ears. Be nice and polite. Raise your hand and use your quiet voice.

Always remember that you're smart. You're brave and handsome. You're funny and witty. You're a wonderful brother, friend, and human.

I love you so much and hope you have an amazing first day of school and school year.

XOXO,

Sissy

Circa 2008 . . . I am not totally sure . . . I found this precious letter that Raya wrote to Taylor Swift. The picture that was supposed to go with it got lost and I don't think it was ever sent. I thought the sentiment was what mattered. He still loves Taylor Swift. He sings along to her songs. He knows the words but is one word behind. It sorts of sounds like an echo!

Dear Taylor Swift,

Hello, my name is Raya Kellenberger and I'm the one in the blue skirt the other one in the picture is my older sister and younger brother Jonathan. We are all big fans of your music, but mainly my little brother loves you. He has to listen to you every day before school, in the morning, when he takes a bath, and whenever he does he always feels happier. See the unique thing about our brother is that he has downsindrum, which effects the way he is mentally and physically. He told me some day he wants to meet you in person, aned says you will be his girlfriend haha. Jon talks very well for having downsindrum and he also uses signlanguage. HIs favorite song of your is Better then REvenge but he also likes the song Mine. We hope to get tickets and passes to meet you at your next concert for a gift for him! Jon even has posters up in his room because he loves you so much as an artist, but we would all really appreciate it if you took your time to give up pictures and write out aurographs to my brother, myself, and our sister it would mean alot to everyone. Thank you for taking the time to read this letter, even if it isn't really Taylor I still think it's pretty cool that fans can do this so thank you so much.

Sincerely, Raya

4: SCHOOL

When I meet a parent of a child with special needs, the first question I ask is, "What school district do you live in?" It is so important and the cause of many of my sleepless nights. Some districts are known for being more progressive with special education.

When Jonathan was born, we were living in a county that was very rural. It was known for not being up to date on educational requirements for children with special needs. I think the school board tried to save money but in the long run, they ended up with some lawsuits because of the lack of resources.

When Jonathan was two years old, I went to a school board meeting. I had him dressed in a cute onesie and he had his leg braces on. I stood and addressed the board with this tiny little child in my arms—his little legs in braces hanging over my arms—his angelic face with those beautiful almond shaped eyes peering at everyone. I was hoping he would steal their hearts. The board members remained stoic and stone-faced. I said, "When I gave birth to Jonathan, everyone advised me to move out of the district." I begged them to please put money into special education. I didn't want to leave my family. I came from a family of educators in the district. My great-grandmother taught in a one-room schoolhouse. My mother taught high school in the district for 25 years. My dad, Miranda, Raya, and I all went to the same elementary school. I spoke from the heart and it was a teary-eyed moment.

I gave up. I didn't think the archaic thinking of the present school board would change and I could see too many struggles ahead. The kids and I moved to a different county when Jonathan was six. It was only ten minutes from where we lived before. It was not an easy decision, but I am so glad I did. Our new school was

a great district for the girls but, unfortunately, had no Life Skills program for Jonathan. He had to get bussed to a different school. It was a long bus ride especially for a little boy with behavioral issues, who didn't like school. We had some rough mornings getting ready for school. It was a struggle getting him ready and on the bus.

The bus driver was wonderful. She was so patient with all of us! She played his favorite music when he had a good day. She had a huge part in maintaining our sanity. We became lifelong friends.

Even though I felt our move was beneficial, things were not perfect. I still had issues with the school district. I felt that I had to always stay on top of things. I carefully interviewed all therapists and aides that worked with Jonathan. I had to trust that the school system had the same standards. I was very wrong. When Jonathan was in elementary school, someone who worked in his school, called my sister to tell her they that were concerned about Jonathan's behavior. They said he was regressing. This person wanted to remain anonymous to me. She/he was a friend of my sister and wanted me to know about Jonathan's inappropriate behavior. It was a huge wake-up call to me when my sister passed along this information.

I was going through a tough time in my life and let my scrutiny relax. I was struggling a lot with life in general. I felt like I was stuck in quicksand and couldn't get out. Being an adult and making adult decisions for myself and three children was staggering at times. Some days, I wanted to go to bed, throw the covers over my head, and never come out.

Who knew that divorce wasn't as glamorous as at it appeared on TV? Who knew that being a single mother with three kids would be so much harder than I ever imagined. Who knew that I wouldn't be top bachelorette of the year? It turned out that a mother of three school-age children was not a top choice for dating material! When I had a night off, I was usually too tired to put much effort into a relationship anyway. I was really struggling.

Jonathan's behavior was horrible. I found this excerpt from Jonathan's IEP. I believe it was written by his teacher or the special ed director.

> Jonathan's behavior has become a serious problem in all school settings. It interferes with his learning and the learning of others; Inappropriate behaviors begin from the time he gets onto the school van in the morning until he is dropped off at home in the afternoon. Jonathan is in homeroom with an aide. While there, he makes constant noises including snorting, barking like a dog, yelling out, and laughing. He calls other children and adults "butthead." He climbs on and under his desk and runs around the classroom. He touches other students' belongings and tries to throw them on the floor. He sticks his tongue out at the other children. He must often be taken to the Life Skills classroom for the remainder of homeroom.
>
> This behavior continues in the Life Skills classroom. In addition to the above behaviors, he will hit other children and adults for no apparent reason. He knocks things on the floor when he walks past them and kicks them. He throws paper, pencils, crayons, etc. He does not want to work. He will repeatedly yell "no, no, no" when asked to do any work that he does not want to do. He spits on the other children and adults. He sticks his tongue out and licks the other children as well as the tables and papers. He "blows" his nose without a tissue and then wipes it on the table, himself, or other children and adults. During all work times and group times, he continues to make loud and inappropriate sounds such as snorting, yelling, barking, and laughing. He will kick other children and poke at them with his pencil. Whenever these behaviors are occurring,

he is always either laughing or grinning and thinks it is quite funny. He climbs on tables and chairs and tries to stand on them. If another student has something that he wants, he will grab it from them and push them to the ground.

This behavior continues during specials. Special teachers often ask that he be removed from their classroom and returned to the Life Skills classroom.

While at recess, he spits on other children and hits other children. He spits on the playground equipment. He pushes other children down onto the ground. When placed on time out at recess, he kicks the fence, kicks the dirt, and yells and laughs. He tries to run away from the aides at recess.

These behaviors continue in the lunchroom. He will throw food at adults and children. He swings his silverware around and pokes adults and children with it. He will hit the aide who is trying to work with him. He gets out of his seat and lays on the lunch table. He gets out of his seat and runs around the cafeteria and tries to run into the kitchen.

These behaviors occur daily and have become almost constant. When he is in time-out in the hallway, he often continues to make loud and inappropriate noises, laughs loudly, sticks his tongue out at the adult with him and calls them "butthead."

There are also occasions when Jonathan seems to be totally out of control. While in the classroom, he will push chairs very hard across the floor at other adults and children, throw things on the floor, knock things off the walls and tables, and yell. It can be very difficult to get him to calm down.

We are currently in the process of trying to obtain TSS services for Jonathan.

A TSS (Therapeutic Support Staff) is a one-on-one aide for an individual with behavioral issues. They can work with the individual in class, home, or social settings. We didn't get a TSS, but eventually got a one-on-one aide for the classroom.

It was hard for me to believe that Jonathan was that much of a menace. I know I am one of those parents, who thinks, "Never my child!" I went to observe him at recess one time. The aides were standing at a distance from Jonathan and would just yell at him when he misbehaved. I was not happy with this situation. I am no expert, but I didn't think it was an effective approach to his behavior issues. Obviously, it wasn't working. He needed positive reinforcement and to be led by example, not just someone standing there yelling at him. I wanted to scream. I didn't know how to deal with all this—how to go about making this situation better for Jonathan. Something needed to be done.

The teacher didn't want Jonathan to have a one-on-one aide. I am not sure why she didn't think he needed one. My cynical thinking was that she didn't want anyone in her classroom who would know what a bad job she was doing.

Part of Jonathan's behavioral problem was due to his frustration because of his speech clarity. He knew what people are saying, but had trouble verbalizing. He was acting out because of his frustration.

We also had a behavior specialist work with us. I had to put some discipline plans in place. I was allowing Jonathan to misbehave because I felt bad for him. I thought he didn't understand his behavior and what he was doing wrong. I figured out that he knew exactly what was going on! I used 1-2-3 Magic—when you state a consequence if the behavior isn't stopped, then count to three. If they don't comply, you follow through with the consequence. When he knew I meant business, we slowly moved forward.

I had an advocate come from CPArc to his IEP (Individualized Education Plan) meeting. CPArc is an agency that advocates for individuals with special needs. They are knowledgeable about legal matters. They also have educational programs and training for anyone working with individuals with special needs. CPArc is an asset to our community. I called and spoke with Sandy. I gave her some background on Jonathan's issues and a copy of his IEP. I told her the date of his next IEP meeting.

An IEP is a guideline or map for Jonathan's year. We met once a year as a team. The team consisted of me, Jonathan, speech therapist, occupational therapist, career ed rep, special ed teacher, local ed agency rep, regular ed teacher, and our community agency rep. We discussed improvements if he had reached his goals, what services he was receiving, and what areas he needed continued extra instruction with. The IEP stated how much time was allotted for his services . . . physical, occupational, and speech. It declared if the individual was eligible for the extended school year (summer school).

Sandy (from CPArc) attended our meeting and ripped the IEP to shreds . . . literally. The school district was behind with the IEP format. The Special Education director was out of touch with what was going on. Sandy was my hero from that point on. She was so impressive. I think the Special Ed director was a little afraid of her. Yay! Mission accomplished. I could have never done that by myself.

We got Jonathan on track with a one-on-one classroom aide. We also increased his speech therapy time. Having a one-on-one aide by his side made him accountable for his actions. He needed someone who was gentle but firm. He needed consistency and positive reinforcement. We put a behavior plan in action and the one-on-one aide could keep track of his actions and behaviors.

I started him on a small dose of Adderall (for ADD-Attention Deficit Disorder). I didn't jump on that bandwagon right away. I asked many professionals what their opinions were. I received many opinions before I made my decision. It turned out to be a good decision (thank goodness).

Another interesting event that occurred at this awful elementary school was Jonathan being sent to the principal's office for swearing! I even received a note that was sent home. He must have been in second grade at the time. He was accused of saying the "F" word. Now, keep in mind that speech is a huge problem for him. Even to this day, he has trouble with Fs. I do swear, but do not use that language in front of the kids. I was floored. For one thing, if they got him to say f . . . why not use it for other words . . . firetruck, fire, four? There are many possibilities! Another thing is that Jonathan did not learn a lesson from going to the principal's office. He was glad to get out of the classroom and visit with the principal. The principal was a family acquaintance and was nice to Jonathan.

Jonathan was stuck on the term butthead for a while. He liked to call everyone a butthead! The special education director told me that she used to have another little boy with Down syndrome who said butthead all the time. The best thing to do is say, "No butthead, say buddy instead." I guess I should have talked to her about the alleged swearing incident.

Then, he moved on to calling people "bad dog." Everyone was a bad dog. Then it was "grouch." Some people don't appreciate being called a grouch! Then, everyone was a "bro." Then, everyone was "Bob." There are a lot of people with the name of Bob. He tries to be funny and likes to make people laugh. Then he just keeps on going when people laugh at his antics. I worry that he is getting too old to be so silly. We all need some silliness, but I think there is a fine line between hearty laughter and overdoing it.

He would forget about the word that was so annoying when he "ran out of steam" with it. When people wouldn't laugh anymore and ignore him, he would stop saying it. He had stopped saying bad dog for a while, thank goodness. Then, we were at the Special Olympics and we ran into an aide from his previous classroom. She said, "Is he still saying Bad Dog?" He heard her and it started all over again. So frustrating. I brought that up at his IEP meeting. I thought the aides would have a little more tactfulness.

For the last two years of Jonathan's middle school experience, he went to a great school with an awesome teacher. That is Mrs. S, you will hear more about her later. We had a wonderful experience. It is such a winning combination to have a good school and a good, caring teacher.

As of this writing, Jonathan is in a Life Skills classroom in high school. A Life Skills class teaches not only academics but also skills to prepare the students for life after school. They are involved in many community activities. His teacher is incredible. Mrs. D has a big class but keeps everyone on task. She texts us and e-mails us for events coming up in the classroom and activities the students are attending. She even e-mails us information she thinks we might be interested in . . . workshops, classes we might like, camps, and dances. I can't believe all the organizational skills that woman possesses.

The nice part is that at the Special Olympics, Mrs. D and all the aides hang out together. Everyone gets along. I feel like a part of a great work of art! The classroom aides truly love their jobs and the students. That is a sign of good management on Mrs. D's part.

I thought that moving to a bigger area, from our rural area, would mean that I was giving up all the "small townness." Everybody knew everybody and knew my parents and siblings and so on. I was pleasantly surprised. Because Jonathan's classroom does so many community projects, people know him everywhere we go. His classroom goes to the grocery store every week. When Jonathan and I go grocery shopping, people say hello and talk to him because they know him from coming in and grocery shopping with his class.

The high school has a club named PALS. It is comprised of kids from Jonathan's classroom and kids from the 'regular' classrooms. They do activities like making crafts, baking cookies, science fair projects, movies, and game night. They make their own matching shirts, too. When Jonathan and I go to the mall, people will say hi and talk to Jonathan. It is because of the PALS club that he knows so many people. They also have a "Coffee Friday" every Friday morning in their Life Skills classroom. It is set up like a business, where teachers and parents can come in and get a coffee and a pastry. The students rotate their responsibilities every week. It is a great learning tool. It makes them hone their skills and socialize. I go to "Coffee Friday" every couple of weeks. Miranda goes along sometimes. My niece, Lydia, and even Grammy have gone. Jonathan takes his job seriously, but when I bring someone along with me, it really perks him up. He acts like he's "big stuff."

Some of the teachers go in every week. They converse with the students and everyone acts professionally. Jonathan has nicknames for a couple of the teachers. He calls one male teacher Ernie and another one Bob—surprise, surprise.

Jonathan's classroom has a special prom, which is a huge deal. Our school works together with three other schools to plan it. Each year, a different school hosts. The host school does the planning and picks a theme. Then, they decorate accordingly. It's an all-day affair with a served lunch. I think lunch is the only time Jonathan sits down! He is up dancing the whole time. He wears his suit and the girls wear fancy dresses. Even the staff dresses up. It is a huge gala event. He loves wearing his suit and tie. I even went all out and bought him dress shoes like he wore in Clay and Miranda's wedding.

The parents go from 9:00–9:30 to take pictures. Miranda went with me one year. She stayed overnight and thought she would make the day extra special and make Jonathan homemade gluten-free cinnamon buns the morning of the prom. She went to a lot of work and he was not impressed! He wanted what he always has every morning.

We leave after picture taking, then the students take a bus to the church where the prom is held. I wanted to go sneak a peek at Jonathan at the prom, but Miranda talked me out of it. He would be mortified if he saw me there. It is his time to shine.

He is also "helping" (I use the term very loosely) the varsity girls' basketball team. He doesn't help much, but he sits behind the team during games. The coach's son sits with him and keeps an eye on him. Jonathan absolutely loves it. He can't wait to go to the games. He calls the coach's son his friend. The coach has assured me that they love having Jonathan around. All the students talk to him and make him feel very important. I tried to sit with him during a game and he told me to "Shoo"!

5: TEACHERS

Jonathan's academic career formally began with preschool at the IU (Intermediate Unit). It was a preschool setting but set up so Jonathan's therapists came there to see him. He had speech, physical, and occupational therapy one time per week. The speech therapist worked on receptive (understanding) and expressive (speaking) language. The physical therapist worked on gross motor skills (jumping, coordination, etc.) and the occupational therapist worked on fine motor skills (holding a pencil, snaps, buttoning, etc.).

We enrolled Raya at this preschool also. It was open to the public. They went together for one year. It was a great beginning for both.

Then, Raya went to kindergarten and Jonathan stayed at preschool. Miranda and Raya had the same wonderful kindergarten teacher. They really loved her. We all loved her. It was a good experience for all of us. I had my mind set on Jonathan going to the same kindergarten and then we would figure out where he should go from there. I knew he wouldn't be in a 'regular' classroom like the girls were, but I thought he would be in 'regular' kindergarten.

We had placement meetings. My friend went with us. She used to babysit the kids and was a good advocate for Jonathan. I would always get befuddled and emotional at any kind of meeting that involved Jonathan's future. I was glad she could be there with me. She pleaded for them to just let us try a regular classroom for kindergarten. The speech therapist and IU teacher wanted him to go to a Life Skills classroom. They were very adamant about this. I had visions of him being included in some regular classes. I spoke to our beloved kindergarten teacher. When I asked her if she would be ok with him in her classroom, she said, "but what would I be able to teach him?" I was crushed. That was one of my first blasts of reality. It felt like a bucket of cold water was thrown in my face.

Jonathan was placed in a Life Skills kindergarten classroom. It was not just kindergarten age children. It was grades kindergarten through third, I believe. I don't think he learned a thing. Maybe, part of my opinion about the lack of academic achievement was based on my discouragement over not getting my own way. We moved out of the county after that first year.

We have been fortunate to have had three great, wonderful teachers—one in elementary school, one in middle school, and one in high school. Students with special needs can attend school until the age of 21. We had some wasted years until we found the right fit for him.

Jonathan went to an elementary school for several years that just wasn't working for him. The teacher was new to special education and seemed unsure of herself and her decisions. There was a lot of tension in the classroom between the aides, teacher, and parents (well, mainly me. I'm not sure how the other parents felt, but I was not happy). That was when he had regression and behavioral issues. We got a one-on-one classroom aide for him, but I felt that a lot of time was wasted. She even fought me to get the one-on-one aide, but I pushed for it.

Then, I discovered a different elementary school in the same district. The teacher was wonderful. I'm not sure if someone was keeping her a secret or what! Apparently, the special education director wasn't allowed to tell me who had better qualifications. I had to figure it out on my own.

We had two wonderful years with this teacher. We were getting Jonathan's behavior under control and he could concentrate on learning. She didn't tolerate any gossip in her classroom between the aides. It was tension-free and a joy to visit the classroom.

Then, Jonathan had to advance to middle school. We had two bad experiences there. The first year, the teacher was inexperienced and too easy going. I heard that one of her students got lost in the hallway one time.

The administration replaced her with a teacher who really pushed academics. The life skills program was supposed to get better academic ratings. She gave him homework that was impossible for him to do. Everything was academically too hard for him. I appreciate having high standards for him, but not impossible goals to reach.

I felt that this teacher didn't like his one-on-one aide and we never really clicked. I dreaded having meetings with her. I remembered one time, I told her that he would be swimming in the annual Special Olympics instead of doing track and field events.

She said, "We can't do that because they need to be timed and they need separate transportation."

I said, "Well, he has been timed and I will take him to the field house where the pool is. He has been taking lessons with Special Olympics for several months." She had no clue what was going on in any of her students' lives.

Afterward, she asked what he wore.

I said, "not a Speedo if that's what you are getting at!" I didn't think that was appropriate at all and it was too late for her to make amends with me. Jonathan and I were both miserable. He hated going to school. I couldn't wait for the school year to be over.

The next year, I switched schools to a middle school that was closer to home. We had a phenomenal experience. My whole family loved Mrs. S. Jonathan adored her. What a difference in our lives. Jonathan loved going to school. She took Jonathan under her wing. She really wanted to teach him to read. She even showed me the book that he would read first.

Mrs. S knew how much Jonathan loved playing basketball, so she arranged for him to manage the junior high basketball team. She would stay with him at practice and bring him home afterward if we weren't there to pick him up. I asked her why she did all of this and she replied, "I like to do it. It's my way of giving." Jonathan felt so special.

We had two wonderful years with her. Jonathan didn't learn to read, but he grew in so many ways. His speech and self-confidence improved. I didn't want to leave her, but Jonathan had to go to high school. He wasn't allowed to stay in middle school forever! I wanted to hold on to her leg, like a little kid and beg her to move to the high school with us.

Mrs. S and I had many conversations concerning Jonathan's placement in high school. It would be a huge change for him. I was ready for a change in my life also. Miranda was in college. Raya had graduated from high school and was getting ready for college. We discussed all the options as a family. We made the decision that we would move—really move. It would be 45-50 minutes away. I would be closer to my work and Jonathan would be going to a school district with a great reputation for its Life Skills classroom.

It was so scary to even think about. I hated moving away from my mom and dad. I was worried about needing help with Jonathan when I was working. I prayed about it a lot. It's very comforting to know that God takes care of us. Everything worked out beautifully. We had a few glitches with caregivers at first, for Jonathan, but it was a good move for us.

Jonathan's first year of high school was an adjustment period. I knew it would be, wherever we decided to go. The classroom was bigger at the high school and had more students. He mostly stayed in the Life Skills classroom. He went out for specials (pottery, computer, and phys. ed).

Whenever Jonathan has an appointment, I send a note along with him to give to Mrs. D. It gives the time I will be picking him up and the reason for early dismissal. I knew Jonathan was having a rough start to his new school when he would show me notes that he made up to hopefully get him out of school early. One morning, he sat at the kitchen table for breakfast. He was writing on a piece of paper. When I asked what he was writing he said, "No school. School closed." Now, he loves school and hates to miss any. When I hand him a note to give to Mrs. D, for an early dismissal, he tries to crumple it up! Two weeks ago, I went to the school to pick him up for an appointment, and no one knew anything about it. He left the note in his locker.

It was a good move for us both.

6: AIDES

A one-on-one aide is for that one person only. The aide is responsible for keeping the student on task and making sure the student is paying attention. The aide is like a liaison between student and teacher. The first one-on-one aide that Jonathan had was very nice and really cared for him. But, I think it was a trial run for everyone involved. She wanted me to let her know if Jonathan wouldn't be coming to school on days that he was sick. This was back in the days that he was sick a lot. So, if he woke up sick and couldn't go to school, I had to:

1. Text the aide.

2. Call the lunch lady because Jonathan was the only one who got a gluten-free meal and she didn't want to prepare it if he wasn't coming.

3. Text the bus driver, so she wouldn't have to go out of her way to get to our house if he wasn't going to school.

4. Call the doctor . . . depending on how sick he was.

5. Make calls to find someone to watch him . . . my mom, his hab aide, my dad . . . or call off work.

This aide and the teacher didn't see eye to eye, so there was a lot of tension. I know the aide had Jonathan's best interests at heart and I appreciated her being his advocate. But, I felt like I was the monkey in the middle a lot of times. They would each tell me stories about the other one. I was stressed out and not sure what to do with the situation and lack of professionalism.

Our next one-on-one was a gem. She truly loved Jonathan. We had her for several years. She really looked out for Jonathan. I didn't have any worries with her by Jonathan's side. We went through a bad teacher or two together. She would let me know if there was anything going on that I should know about. When the teacher was giving him papers that were too hard for him, she would give him something that he could understand better.

She always got him presents on his birthday and at Christmas. Even when we didn't have her services anymore, she still sent him birthday cards. She would have him over to their house sometimes. She truly loved him. He loved her too. It was sad when he graduated from needing a one-on-one.

I would keep in contact with her after she was done working with Jonathan, and she followed the family's Facebook pages, but of course, it wasn't the same and she missed him. We missed her too. After many months of Jonathan being at school on his own, while on vacation, we ran into her husband and daughter. We arranged to stop at their campsite and surprise her. It worked. She was so surprised and excited to see Jonathan that she started crying.

The teacher decided that he didn't need a one-on-one anymore. She didn't want him to become dependent on the aide. I didn't feel comfortable having him in her classroom without an aide. Although he may not have needed an aide for behavior, his lack of verbal communication concerned me. It would be very easy for him to get accused of something and not be able to handle the situation. Or another scary scenario was that if something bad happened to him at school he wouldn't be able to tell me about it. Having an aide was a huge comfort for me. I knew details of his everyday schedule. He really couldn't get in trouble because she was constantly with him, making sure he was behaving. I disagreed and had the advocate from CPArc come to the IEP meeting. She tried to discuss the options, but the teacher and special education director held firm.

I didn't realize it at the time, but it was a blessing in disguise. I decided to change schools and found Mrs. S. He didn't need a one-on-one aide in her classroom. Thank you, God.

Recently, Jonathan's classroom aide (he no longer needs a one-on-one) told me that she is a better person because of Jonathan. They love him. I am so blessed. They buy him lunch at Special Olympics if he doesn't have one (because honestly, I may have forgotten to pack it a time or two). They said they do it because they love him.

As part of Jonathan's services, he has a Hab aide for a few hours a week. A Hab aide is responsible for getting Jonathan out and active in the community. We have goals and objectives for him to work toward. We meet with the supports coordinator once a month to make sure everything is going okay.

One of the goals we had listed was Safety. Jonathan used to dart out of the car and around parking lots without looking. This was a huge concern. He had to learn to hold hands and watch for traffic before crossing streets. He learned what a STOP sign meant. Now anytime I pull up to a stop sign, he puts his palm out and shouts "STOP!"

Another goal was Manners. This is very important to me. I want him to say please and thank-you and can conduct himself appropriately in public. His aide takes him out to eat and he learns how to order food for himself and behave in public.

Third was Household Chores. As part of the push toward his independence, he works on cleaning and cooking. He cannot use the stove without assistance. He can use the microwave, though. Mrs. D made him a chart to use. We have the chart on the refrigerator beside the microwave. It lists the steps he needs to use the microwave. The chart states pressing twenty seconds and that's what he does! Sometimes, it takes a lot of twenty seconds to heat up his food, but that is ok.

He helps me with the dishes, folds laundry and vacuums. He enjoys vacuuming and folding clothes and will do that without much prompting. He needs to be prompted to help with dishes. All I must do is threaten him with Bert and Ernie. He loves to watch them on YouTube. When I say, "no Bert and Ernie if you don't help," he is right there.

My niece, Lydia, watched him one time. She said it was the easiest babysitting job ever. After he ate, he took his dish to the sink and washed it, without her telling him to do that!

Another goal was Social Skills. Let's face it, we all have issues at times, socially. He likes to make people laugh. If they laugh, he continues, and continues, and continues. He calls everyone Bob or tries to tickle them. He has come a long way. He used to be all over the place when we would go out to eat. Now, he sits very nicely. He inhales his food, but has his napkin on his lap! One night, we were eating at a restaurant and I looked over at him. He had a whole lettuce leaf hanging out of his mouth . . . half in and half out. The table manners are a work in progress, but at least he eats healthily! And, you know, lettuce is so hard to cut sometimes!

Then there's Using Money in public places. He has a wallet and some money, but he has a hard time with the concept of money. At Christmas time, he and his aide go shopping for the family. We make a list, and he has a certain amount that he can spend. Jonathan needs help with handling money.

We had the same hab aide for many years. Susan became part of the family. I probably couldn't have worked if I hadn't trusted her so wholeheartedly. She helped us out when he was sick and when I was sick. She even went to some doctor's appointments with us.

Susan treated Jonathan as her own. He was part of her family. He loved going to her house to play with her grandkids and do activities with them. It was hard to find community activities in our rural area, but they were always busy. She took him to Community Aide, the library, on walks, and out to eat.

Susan even went on vacation with us. One year, I rented a place in Virginia Beach for a week. She wanted to drive separately and meet us there a day later. I packed up the van myself (a huge mistake)! I thought I was so clever. I even tied a box of Jonathan's toys on top of the van. Well, of course, the box didn't stay tied to the top of the van and flew out and all over the road. This happened before we left town! I was just running an errand before we left. I was so disgusted and upset. I picked up what I could and left everything at home. We got to Virginia Beach with no beach toys or stuff for Jonathan to do.

When Susan got there, she took him to the Community Aide and bought him some stuff to play with. We had a nice vacation, once we got there. She saved the day again! Susan also went to Disney with us. I never could have managed to take that trip and do things without her help. The kids were in tenth, fifth, and third grades. We went in November. It was a great time of year to go, but the kids had to miss school for a week.

Miranda likes wild rides. Since she was older and much taller, she could go on the bigger rides. So, I would go with her. At least I attempted to go with her, but after I made myself sick on Space Mountain, I just waited in line with her.

Susan would take Raya and Jonathan on the smaller, less crazy rides. Raya gets motion sickness, so she's not big on rides. Jonathan loves rides and was happy riding whatever he could. It worked out well. We would meet up every couple of hours and regroup.

It was a wonderful family vacation, thanks to Susan. She even gave me a picture collage to remember it. It is a treasured picture.

Our time with Susan ended after many good memories and years of her caring for Jonathan. We had a scheduling conflict. Jonathan was interested in basketball after school. It would make her days too late. I had to start the search again for a hab aide for Jonathan.

A friend of mine worked as his hab aide for a few months. That was nice. He was part of her family and we were neighbors. It was convenient for Jonathan and me. Sadly, we lost her also. She had another job and a family. We also had scheduling conflicts.

Then, my brother was his aide. My brother was a wrestler for many years. He was a teacher and a wrestling coach. My brother, Bryon, is the fun uncle. All the nieces and nephews love to roughhouse with him. So Jonathan felt special that he got the one-on-one attention of Uncle Bryon. Bryon took his new position seriously. He worked with Jonathan's speech. They even worked out together. Jonathan really enjoyed his guy time and doing guy things for a change.

One time, Bryon was getting Jonathan off the bus and the bus driver (not my friend) told Bryon that Jonathan made a racist comment to another student on the bus. Bryon was surprised and said, "You can say many things about my sister and Jonathan's behavior, but she is not racist and doesn't make racist comments. You realize she has a daughter from China?"

I called the bus driver and she said that she couldn't understand what he said, but she didn't think it was nice. I knew that Jonathan acts goofy and gets on the other kids' nerves. I wondered if that's what the problem was. The bus driver said she would have to report it to the teacher.

Bryon and I talked to Jonathan. We told him not to make fun of people because he doesn't like it when people make fun of him. I told the bus driver to let me know if the comments continued. She said that she decided she must have misunderstood him and didn't report it to the teacher because his computer privileges would be taken away. I talked to the teacher anyway. I wanted to make sure he was behaving in her classroom. She assured me that he never made racist comments in her classroom.

When we moved, I had trouble transferring the paperwork and getting a new aide. I was stressed beyond belief. I desperately needed help with him after school. I contacted local high schools and colleges. My friends' daughter stayed with us and helped, but she also had a job. Miranda was interning and had a time conflict. Raya went away to college in New York.

There were so many changes going on, and I wasn't dealing with it very well. Sometimes, I would try to take off work, race home, get Jonathan off the bus, and take him back to work with me. This was stressful because if I was running late, I would give myself a stress headache, worrying about getting there on time. He panics when no one is there for him. Even for a small amount of time, he can't be alone. Sometimes, I would pick him up early at school, over my lunch hour and take him to work with me for the afternoon. I had the bus drop him off at my office one time. They dropped him off at the orthodontist office across the street! It was no big deal, because, luckily, he was a patient at that orthodontist office. They looked at him when he walked in, looked at the schedule and realized he didn't have an appointment. He was just playing with some of their games. The girls, that worked there, called our office and wondered if we were looking for Jonathan. Marty walked over to get him.

I had to make many phone calls to see why our paperwork wasn't transferring. I can make phone calls if I get a break between patients and over my lunchtime, but it is hard to receive return phone calls when I am with a patient. This prolonged the process even more. The different counties needed different paperwork and additional testing. Jonathan needed another psych evaluation. We had meetings and phone calls and phone calls and meetings. Finally, after four months without any services, our prayers were answered.

We met our aide. His name was Anthony. I wasn't sure about Anthony at first, an older man, that I didn't know with my son in my home. My uncertainty was short-lived. He was a retired basketball coach—very active and loved Jonathan. They hit it off right away.

I was worried at first about having the house in shape and would get up early to straighten up because I didn't know Anthony and didn't want him to think I was a terrible housekeeper. Now, Anthony is a part of the household. He sees every sink full of dirty dishes. Anthony is retired, so he is available whenever Jonathan has off school for the day if school lets out early, and all summer long. He schedules his summer vacation around Jonathan's calendar. They do all kinds of things together. Anthony stands by while Jonathan makes his bed every day and puts his clothes away. They go to movies, out to eat, and shopping. They also play basketball, go for walks, go to the playground, and work on academics. Jonathan is a part of his family, too. Anthony even took Jonathan to his Bible School. Jonathan helped with the little kids and really liked it. And of course, they play basketball! I mentioned earlier that Jonathan helped with the high school varsity girls' basketball team. It is Anthony that took him and I think he enjoyed it as much as Jonathan did!

Every year for Christmas, Jonathan wants to get Anthony a basketball. I'm not sure how many basketballs one guy can have!

We are so fortunate and grateful to have Anthony. He even took Jonathan to open house at the school. The teachers and classroom aides were glad to meet Anthony. They had heard so much about him.

7: LIFE

I am so grateful every day for what I have. Jonathan has taught me so much about life. Anyone who has a chance to get to know him learns what a precious gift he is.

> *October 1998*
> They say that God works in mysterious ways, but there seems to be no mystery with our sweet little boy. He was sent to bring an answer to your prayers for a baby. The mystery of why he has Down syndrome is insignificant. His life was meant to be your life. And maybe the mystery was who would be so blessed to receive the gift of Jonathan.

When Jonathan was approximately two years old, he started to roll cans. This went on for several years. He would take the cans out of the cupboard and line them up and roll them from room to room. He had a specific order he used. Raya would like to take a can out of his line up and he had a fit. He knew where each can belonged in his sequence.

After a while, the labels would come off the cans and get thrown away. We had "guessing game" meals. We would all take a guess at what was in the can. Was it peaches or green beans?! It was the joke in the family that if you were hungry, lift the sofa because there are bound to be some cans under there!

Somehow Jonathan got a hold of a glass jar of spaghetti sauce. He took it to the second floor and decided to let it drop, not roll. He dropped it over a ledge we had in the hallway. It fell straight down to the first floor and shattered. There was broken glass and spaghetti sauce everywhere! It looked like a murder scene!

When Jonathan was fourteen years old, we were shopping on Thanksgiving weekend. He found a Wii game that he really wanted. It was a Sesame Street music game. I bought it but told him that he couldn't have it until Christmas. He asked several times for it (he doesn't let go of anything quickly). I told him, "no, not until Christmas." I know . . . hard to believe I can say no to him!

Early the next morning, Jonathan went downstairs to my storage room. I couldn't figure out what he was doing. Soon, he came upstairs with Christmas wrapping paper. He proceeded to wrap the Wii tape with the Christmas paper. He made me go back to bed and pretend to sleep. Then, he "woke me up" saying, "Morning, Ho ho ho." To Jonathan, "Ho ho ho" means Santa Claus. He wanted to pretend it was Christmas, so he could open his present!

He never ceases to amaze me. My life is so full of humbling and heartfelt moments because of him. One thing I resented and still do is that everyone makes assumptions or stereotypes about Jonathan. When Jonathan was born, they assumed he had heart trouble because 60% of children with Down syndrome do. I am glad we proved them wrong. Although, we discovered his heart troubles a few years later.

Kids with Down syndrome are individuals too. Everyone says, "Aw, they are so loving. They are so sweet," as if they are alike in that way. Well, Jonathan is Jonathan. He is a great little guy with Down syndrome. They would not think he was so sweet if they would see him when he does not get his own way. He can be very stubborn and persistent!

There are many benefits to having a child with special needs. To see holidays and special events through his eyes makes every occasion or event extra special. His Halloween costume is always a big deal. We start looking for it at the beginning of October. A friend of mine from work has handmade many costumes for him. He loves them and would sleep in them if I would let him. He will even wear old costumes around the house, even if they are too small. He has been Kung Fu Panda, Oscar the Grouch and a minion.

Our town hosts a Halloween parade. People dress up, typically in big group themes, and throw candy as they walk down the street. People line up all along the sidewalk, even bringing chairs. When they throw candy, Jonathan doesn't run to get it. He just stands where he is, watching the candy fall and the people pass. We told him to grab the candy. Still, he stood. Miranda and Clay grabbed him by the hands to show him how but he would wiggle out. After

a few signs and words, we realized that Jonathan wasn't picking up the candy because he didn't want to go off the sidewalk and onto the road. Five years ago, he wouldn't have thought twice about running into the middle of the street and now he can't even be lured off the sidewalk with delicious candies! Things tend to be black and white with Jonathan.

Three or four years ago, he was Kung Fu Panda. It was an adorable costume, but it was huge! He absolutely loved it. We went to my friend's house for a Halloween party. Her house was warm and his costume was heavy. He would not take it off and was sweating! I finally told him to go outside to cool off. A few minutes later, I went outside to check on him and he was laying on her chaise with his costume on. Kung Fu's belly was sticking way out to the side. It was hysterical to see, but he would not take off that costume.

Two years ago, when he was seventeen, he went as Kung Fu Panda again, but the costume was getting too small. Miranda and I took him trick or treating. He couldn't move his legs, because the costume was tight. So, he would teeter to each side and hop up on the step at the front door because he wouldn't move his legs enough to step up normally! Miranda and I laughed and laughed. We had to be careful and watch him, so he didn't tip over! This year he wanted to be a pirate minion. I bought an eye patch and a plastic 'hook' hand. He already had the minion costume.

He likes to go trick or treating. He doesn't have much interest in the candy but likes to go to the houses. It's good socialization for him. He knows the rule is that he must tell everyone "thank you," and this year he added something to his routine. He would hook everyone with his plastic hook hand. He gently grabbed their arm with his hook. Little old ladies thought it was cute, but men just tried to shake his hook, like you would a hand. One house we went to had a little boy dressed up like a pirate. He and Jonathan really 'shook hooks!' He really loved that hook.

Christmas is over the top. Jonathan loves to decorate and sing and tell me what he wants "Ho ho ho" to bring him. Raya asked me a couple of years ago when we were going to tell him there's not really a Santa Claus.

I said, "Why would we ruin that for him, for us?" His look on Christmas morning is priceless. I am trying to get him into the giving part of Christmas also. He does like to wrap presents and buy people presents.

I always dressed the kids in matching outfits for Christmas pictures. The funny thing is, I still buy matching shirts or pajama bottoms every year. On Christmas Eve, whoever is at our house and staying over (Grammy, Miranda, Clay, Raya, and Jonathan) must open their special gift. Then we all wear them and take a group picture. We love Christmas!

Birthdays are so exciting for Jonathan. He loves to party! The problem is he thinks everyone's birthday is his. He even cried one time at school because it was someone else's birthday.

We had a surprise party for Jonathan's sixteenth birthday. I wasn't sure how he would do. He always talks about surprises and tries to surprise us all the time. But, I wasn't sure how he would react when he was the one being surprised.

He walked in with Miranda and Clay and was totally surprised. He was shy and awkward for a little, then got into the party. There was only one boy from his class, one family friend, and the rest were family members.

We made some of his favorite foods: hot dogs, baked beans, barbecue, chips, and a gluten-free cake. Everything was gluten-free. We don't always do that because not everyone likes gluten-free cake, etc., but on his birthday, it's his day!

His eighteenth birthday just happened to fall on the weekend of Miranda's graduation from Saint Francis University. The graduation ceremony was on a Sunday. The day before the school

held a smaller awards ceremony just for the Occupational Therapy Program. There were approximately forty graduates in the class.

After the ceremony, the class and professors went outside for pictures. They were all in perfect formation and broke out in song. They all sang "Happy Birthday" to Jonathan. Miranda had arranged for all the graduates to sing to him! I thought he might be embarrassed, but instead, he started to dance! I, of course, had to wipe away a tear. Miranda spent the previous night baking gluten-free cupcakes for him. She invited friends over to our table to eat them and Jonathan graciously handed out cupcakes and napkins.

We went to a family member's' birthday party one summer day. Jonathan was fourteen. The birthday boy was five or six. There were lots of little kids playing. Jonathan seemed like he was on the outside wanting to be part of the action. Sometimes, he doesn't know how to fit in. He is tall like an older kid but thinks like a younger kid.

Sometimes, he does goofy things to try to get a laugh. Sometimes, he would push or act out to get attention. I try to play with him, but he doesn't want his mother to be the one playing with him. He wants to play with the kids. My heart aches for him. Because of his delayed speech, it is hard for kids to understand him. You must be around him for a while to really understand and sometimes, I don't even get it.

The kids had squirt guns and there weren't enough to go around. The kids were not sharing. I told Jonathan to use the sprinkler for a squirt gun. I had seen the other kids doing this. What I didn't realize was that the other kids were hiding their sprinkler usage from the parents. They were much sneakier than Jonathan. He got yelled at for playing with the sprinkler. He was so upset. I got mad, grabbed Jonathan and left in tears. I took Jonathan to my brother's house, where he played in the pond with my brother and his friends. The big boys were very sweet to Jonathan. Every now and then, I have a meltdown. Sometimes, I feel like I can't deal with the ignorance and lack of compassion any longer. Sometimes, I wish people would try harder to understand Jonathan and to get to know him. One good thing that happened because of that day was that my step-mother gave us a bag of toys and squirt guns to keep in the car so that he would never be without one again.

We were at a family wedding. Jonathan was still in his bad behavior stage. He would be on the dance floor and before I knew it, he was gone. I thought his sisters were watching him, then they would get distracted and off he would go. He was all over this huge venue. I was really struggling.

An employee yelled at me that he was out of control. He had even been in the kitchen. Times like this, I felt so beaten-down, so awful. I feel like I am a terrible person and mother. I left in tears again.

> *June 12, 1998*
>
> Eve,
>
> It is not Jonathan who needs support and reassurance. You are the one who must take a frightening path with so many new things to learn about parenting a child with Down syndrome.
>
> And when I cry for this situation, I realize I am crying for you. It only takes a look at Jonathan to know that he will thrive. He will have a good life . . . be happy . . . and enjoy a carefree life. You, however, must learn and change and adjust and . . .

Jonathan and I walked into the grocery store. He was fourteen years old. He brought his stuffed Woody doll (from *Toy Story*) along and put him in the toddler seat in the cart! The store was crowded because it was Friday. Everyone was doing paycheck Friday grocery shopping.

Jonathan likes to push the cart by himself. It makes him feel very important and independent. He was trying so hard to be careful and maneuver our cart between other carts without hitting anyone or their cart. He was concentrating so hard. I was trying to be patient. This was very important to him. When he got to the end of an aisle successfully, he said, "I did it." He was so proud of his accomplishment. I was too. I said, "great job buddy." We exchanged high fives. The reward for doing a good job in the grocery store was going to the library. He wanted to get five turtle books (Franklin). The line was very long at the checkout. I kept reminding him about the library and added that maybe we could have a picnic for our lunch. He was very excited about that prospect.

The cashier was staring at him. I assumed it was because she didn't understand what he was saying. I try to ignore the stares. Every item he pulled out of the cart and placed on the counter, he asked if it's for our picnic. I tried so hard to be patient and answer him yes or no. He will typically repeat himself until I answer him. When he held up the toilet paper and asked if it was for the picnic, I jokingly said, "That is NOT for the picnic." That got a chuckle out of everyone, Jonathan included!

Then, we got to the car. He helped me by unloading the cart. I opened the back and he noticed some things that were already there—an umbrella, a pair of shoes, some books. He had to rearrange them. Everything must be just right.

He asked whether each bag as he placed them in the car from the cart if it was for the picnic. My patience was wearing thin. It was very hot and humid outside and I was getting a headache. A short trip to the grocery store had taken a lot longer than I planned.

Jonathan has always liked to put the cart away. He's pretty good at it, but I still watch him carefully. He might forget to watch for cars and dart across the parking lot in his excitement for his upcoming library trip and picnic.

He was so good once we got to the library. He just sat there and looked at books. It was a hard decision for him to only pick five books. He usually talks me into getting six. My patience was restored. He loves to look at books and it keeps him occupied for a long time. We had a wonderful picnic.

Every year, our family has a huge kayaking trip on the Fourth of July weekend. It started with just a few people and one overnight camping excursion on my brother's property. It has now grown to probably about 50 people and as many as three nights on my cousin's property. They made a little camping area along the river, complete with a pavilion and porta potty. It is a great place to have a family reunion. We have great food, fishing, and fun and games. Jonathan loves playing ball and Frisbee with the big guys—my cousin's friends are wonderful to Jonathan.

We had gone to the party portion of the festivities to see my relatives and family friends, but in the past, were never able to go on the kayaking excursions. Jonathan always wanted to, but I didn't feel that he could handle a kayak himself. Sometimes the river can be fast, especially if there is a lot of rain. In the past, I tried kayaking with him in the same kayak with me and we did it for several miles, but it was very uncomfortable. We ended up dumping over and got very wet. Miranda tried this as well and while it worked to her advantage initially (he would paddle her around), she soon became frustrated. Single person kayaks are not built for two people and it becomes very difficult.

This past Fourth of July, we were so excited. We planned a two-day kayak trip with everyone else. I rented a tandem kayak (made for two people), made a special patriotic dessert, and packed our bags. I even bought matching red, white, and blue shirts (my kids will never be too old for me to make them wear matching shirts)!

My brother, thoughtfully, got Jonathan a special straw hat, just like his, to wear on the kayak. We had so much fun. Jonathan really got the hang of paddling and even let me relax and talk to my sisters when we caught up with them.

After the trip down the river, it stormed badly. My mom lives close to the reunion location, so we went there to get out of the rain.

Then it was time for the big party. We took lots of pictures. My dad, aunt, and uncle were all there. I have five brothers and sisters. We were all there. It was a great reunion.

As the darkness grew, lanterns were lit. There was a fire down by the river, but it was still dark. The river wasn't too far away, just down a slope. Some people were fishing and hanging out down there. The rest of us were up top where all the food and fireworks were. I was sitting, chatting, and letting Jonathan do his own thing. He was always looking for someone to play ball or Frisbee with. Suddenly, I realized I couldn't see Jonathan. I panicked a little. I walked around asking if anyone had seen him. Then I started panicking more. I asked Miranda if she knew where he was. She had no idea. Then I panicked a lot. I was starting down the slope toward the river, yelling his name. I am sure I sounded like an insane mother. Then, I heard this little voice, "Mom, right here." He was sitting in a lawn chair under the pavilion, like a civilized human being with a bunch of other people. It is hard for me to relax!

We went to my mom's (Grammy) to spend the night. I am not a camper anymore. The next morning, we got up and went to the river at the designated time, only to discover there was no tandem kayak for us. We were beyond disappointed. I thought I had planned so carefully. There was a definite lack of communication. I was scrambling, trying to think what I can do to make this up to Jonathan. I got so disgusted with myself and others. It seems as if things aren't as easy for us as they are for others. We can't just jump in a kayak and go. Sometimes, I feel like, as a mother of a child with special needs, I should make extra arrangements or have a backup plan. Jonathan likes to know every detail of our plans and it's not easy to change plans at the last minute.

We ended up taking Grammy for lunch at a Chinese place. That was a treat for all three of us. Then, we went swimming at Miranda and Clay's. We salvaged the day.

8: MY LIFE

My life has taken on new meaning. I fight for things that I never even knew about before. I rejoice in things that used to seem so small and meaningless. I have learned to appreciate small milestones and improvements that I have taken for granted.

Although, sometimes, I feel so sorry for myself. When I am visiting with friends . . . I feel like I have so little to contribute to the conversation. They are remodeling their homes and planning vacations. My thought process is more like . . . can I make payments on a hearing aid . . . did I make all the phone calls I was supposed to, during my lunch hour, can I run to the pharmacy? Don't get me wrong, I am so grateful for my healthy, wonderful family. I just feel like an outsider sometimes. I am at such a different place in my life than my friends and family. I have worked a full and part-time jobs to make ends meet. I worked full-time as a Dental Hygienist and part-time as a waitress. I enjoyed the variety of my jobs and I met lots of wonderful people, but it kept me extremely busy. The kids weren't deprived of anything, but I worked hard to make sure of that. I sometimes felt like I was on a see-saw, balancing back and forth, with having enough time to spend with the kids and having enough money to do some fun things.

I miss a lot of work because of doctors' appointments and school functions. It's okay if I can make appointments far enough in advance to ask for time off or the day off. Sometimes, it's hard to find a sub to work for me. A big problem was when one of the kids was sick, and I had to take off work. Being a Dental Hygienist, I felt a responsibility to my patients and my fellow employees. Dental offices don't like it if you call off work frequently. It wreaks havoc with the schedule.

When Jonathan was in elementary school, he had quite a few upper respiratory illnesses. I remember one time, the school nurse called me at work to come and pick him up. He was sick. I left work and picked him up at school and took him back to work. He was too sick to be at school, but not sick enough to go to the doctor's office. My office manager held him while I worked.

Now, I live close to work and Jonathan's school is also nearby. So, if there is a two-hour delay because of snow or ice, I take Jonathan to work with me. We have a lounge area with a TV and couch. He makes himself at home until I can take him to school. Hopefully, a patient will cancel at the time he needs to go. That gives me some time to take him to school and get back to work. I have been seen dashing across the lawn at the school when my time away from work was tight. It usually works out, but one time, I had to take him an hour or two late. I just couldn't get away.

People my age talk about retirement. I won't be able to retire for a long time. A lot of my friends have second homes and new cars. I apply for financial aid to join the YMCA. A second home for me is going to my mom's. She plays and reads to Jonathan so I can relax a little bit.

My mom waits up for us. If we are staying at her house and Jonathan and I are out somewhere having a good time, we must make sure we don't get home to her house too late, because she can't sleep until we are home. This is reminiscent of my teenage years!

My sister and friends go out to hear a band that we love at a local bar. I can't go out unless I have a sitter and I don't always have enough money for that. I can't ask Miranda and Clay all the time to keep Jonathan. I must go to places that are "Jonathan friendly." We can go to my brother's house, so Jonathan can play outside. We can go to my dad's house so he can play basketball. My dad and stepmom also save him magazines to look at. They have a special basket by the back door for his magazines! We can go to my mom's house where he rides his bike around and around and I don't have to be constantly watching him. She lives in the country and doesn't have a street or road to worry about cars. It's a safe environment for him.

We can go to some friends' house if he feels comfortable. It takes him a while sometimes to get adjusted to a different place.

Sometimes, I feel like I am on the outside looking in on someone's life. It's not really my life.

Occasionally, I get sick of being responsible. I want to be the "crazy lady" walking around town in my bathrobe and slippers! (If you see me doing this someday, please offer me a cup of coffee!) I would like to wake up one morning and not have an agenda to be taken care of.

There are always phone calls to make, paperwork to fill out, and appointments to make. It takes me forever to fill out paperwork for Jonathan to go to summer camp. I finally get it sent in (not always on time) and I get an email that I forgot something!

When he first started wearing his neck brace, I forgot to put it on him in the morning. I would go rushing into his school, before work, to put it on his neck. The ladies in his classroom said, "We are going to have to start putting coffee on for you." Not a bad idea! He helps me remember to put his brace on now. When I forget to take out his retainer in the mornings, I find it on the dining room table later . . . ew . . .

I feel like I am always trying to get through one phase and then things will ease up . . . after this round of appointments, we will catch our breath . . . after this busy time at school, we can relax for a while. But, it doesn't seem to ease up. There is always something on my to-do list. As I am writing this, I realize I forgot to call the eye doctor. It seems Jonathan's regular ophthalmologist retired and I was the only person in a three-county radius who didn't know!

Sometimes, I am just so disgusted with my life. I feel like my wheels are spinning and I'm not getting anywhere. Jonathan and I went away for one night. We stayed overnight at a friend's house and had so much fun. Then, we came home and felt like we had double the work. I have so much paperwork to do always. The cat had fleas, the house was a mess, and laundry needed to be done. Everything is so overwhelming sometimes. Everywhere, I looked, something needed to be done. UGH!

Jonathan and I seem to be in the car a lot. We are always going somewhere . . . appointments, the store, visiting people, etc. He loves to change the radio station. He doesn't even wait to see what the next song is, he just keeps moving the stations around until he finds something he likes again. When I am in heavy traffic and getting a little tense, I tell him to not touch the buttons, to just leave it alone. So, if he doesn't approve of the song, he turns down the volume. He will say "no sing!" to me somedays and be upset if I continue to sing along, crossing his arms, tilting his head down, and furrowing his eyebrows. He will point to himself and shout, "me sing!". "Me sing" is easily mistaken for "me king", another common phrase in the car.

A lot of our car time is also spent with Jonathan and his iPad. He has a learning program called Proloquo, which his teacher and speech therapist used to work with him. It is a great communication tool. If I can't understand what he is saying, I ask him to show me on the iPad.

When we are in the car, he likes to have his iPad say words and we repeat them (and repeat them and repeat them . . . repeatedly). It is a great time for us to build his speech and language skills. On more than one occasion, I missed a turn because I was helping him spell something.

Sometimes, I am so mentally tired that my patience is thin. I want to scream and get irritated until I get on the right road again. I look at his sweet cherub face and he asks for a hug. How can I be irritated with him after that? He makes me smile. He gives the best hugs.

I just met a girl with Down syndrome. She is younger than Jonathan but spoke with more clarity and in complete sentences. I feel so bad that maybe I didn't work with Jonathan enough in his formative years. Maybe, when I was going through my divorce, I wasn't paying enough attention to his speech and language needs. Maybe I worked too much. I should have been home more to work on speech and reading.

I try to tell myself that he has other assets . . . and he does. He is handsome, funny, sweet, and great to be with. I know that there is a spectrum with Down syndrome, just like with everything else. Not everyone is at the same place on the spectrum. God created us so that everyone is different. Jonathan is happy, but I know he gets so frustrated when people can't understand him. I'm sorry Jonathan if it's my fault.

I had to sign up Jonathan for OVR. It was on my to-do list for several months. I have to-do lists for small things like making appointments or phone calls. Then, there are the to-do lists for time-consuming things like signing up for OVR and things that I must use the computer to sign up for. I have a mental block for computer work.

My friend asked me if received a confirmation email about a dance for Jonathan. I know I signed up for it. I told her that I was not good with computers. "I will check. Maybe it is in my scam." She said, "Do you mean spam?"

Well, I finally registered Jonathan for OVR yesterday. It wasn't too painful. It only took a couple of reminders from Mrs. D, his teacher. God bless her. I felt so good to cross that task off my list. Whew!

Then, tonight at swimming practice, someone brought up the topic of trust funds for special needs. This a very time-consuming, tedious, and expensive task that needs to be added to the to-do list.

The moms or dads sit on benches outside of the pool room. It is a long hallway with a heater blowing hot, hot air. You can't get away from it. We sit there and sweat for 45 minutes.

We sit and chat or sometimes I close my eyes and pretend I am on a tropical island! Sometimes, I just want to be alone with my thoughts and relax because of a busy day.

Hopefully, my friend Kathleen is there and we can catch up. We usually take turns complaining about something. It's so nice to have a friend that is in the same situation as you are and has a lot of the same issues we are dealing with.

But, tonight at swim practice, the topic was trust funds. Kathleen had been through it and gave us the name of her attorney. All three of us moms got out our pens and papers to jot down the attorney's name and number. It's one of those things that needs to be done, but I keep putting off. Plus, the attorney fees are considerable. Kathleen said it's not fun, but she's glad it's done. One more thing to add to the list. Ugh!

9. DOs AND DON'Ts

DO

1. Be positive. From the beginning, I did not want to hear, "Aw, you poor thing. You have your hands full." Believe me, some days I have enough self-pity. I do not need anyone else's!

When Jonathan was quite small, we were leaving one of his many appointments and my mother told me that she was proud of us. She said, "You have learned so much and come so far." That meant a lot to me and has stuck with me all that time.

My dad tells me from time to time that I am doing a good job with Jonathan . . . that he is a good kid. I need to hear this reassurance every now and then.

Neither one of my parents throw out compliments readily, so these positive words mean a lot.

2. Be patient. Jonathan is not in a hurry to do anything (except eat). It's impossible to get him to hurry up if we are running late for the bus or church. We just must go without brushing teeth or ironing his shirt.

He knows what he is trying to say, it is just hard to express. The more you are around him, the easier it is to understand him. So, one must be very patient when he is trying to speak or else learn sign language. It is a very interesting language. He has taught me a lot. And, please be patient with me. Sometimes, I felt like I ran a marathon before I even got to work! I was exhausted getting three kids out the door in the mornings. For a couple of years, they were going to three different schools! My days off were spent on the phone, planning or appointments or traveling to those appointments. I was frazzled a lot.

This has all gotten a lot better. I only run a 5K before work and spend some of my days off reading or relaxing! (I should be cleaning, but I would rather read!)

3. Be understanding. We have already gone to church and I realize Jonathan's lips are very chapped because he breathes through his mouth a lot. I didn't have any chapstick with me, so I used a little bit of my lip gloss . . . just a tiny bit. It was hardly noticeable! So, please be understanding if Jonathan has issues later in life! It was all my fault!

DON'T

1. Don't ever, ever, ever and I mean never use the "R" word. It's politically incorrect, outdated terminology and it is just plain unacceptable. Do not use this word in context with a person, place, or thing . . . in any situation. It is never appropriate to use.

2. Don't judge Jonathan. Not only because of his learning challenges, but he is my baby and I probably spoil him a little (well, probably a lot)! His sisters think I let him get away with far more than they could get away with! They think I do too much for him and I probably do.

3. Don't judge me. Please, I know I have made mistakes and I wish I had more time to work with Jonathan and his speech. I know I don't always do the right thing, but I try. Sometimes, I feel like I am being watched and judged when we are in public. I know I was when Jonathan was younger and I was having trouble with his behavior. Some lady yelled at me in the grocery store one time. I was humiliated. I am not perfect. I did not read the book on Parenting 101! I am learning as I go.

4. Don't ignore Jonathan. Don't ignore Jonathan just because you don't understand him. He is very hard to understand, especially if you aren't around him very much. He responds to kindness though and loves to hold hands. So, even if you can't understand him, he knows if you are being nice and trying to include him.

One time during the children's sermon, the junior pastor asked everyone, except Jonathan, a question. He probably didn't notice it as much as I did. My family noticed it also. I never said anything in front of Jonathan because he enjoys church and I didn't want him to be discouraged from going. He loves to wear a tie and look nice in church.

When it happened a second time, I was very upset. I just told him he was too big for the children's sermon. It was probably not intentional or maybe she was worried she wouldn't be able to understand him, but I was there to interpret. She should have included him and asked him the question also. He has feelings too.

I think as parents, we all worry about what our kids will say in front of the church. I know I used to sit on pins and needles when Miranda answered questions. Raya talked non-stop. She got yelled at one time by a pastor to be quiet! But it is all part of the children thing. They are unpredictable. Jonathan is just childlike longer than most children.

5. Don't judge my housecleaning (or lack of it)! It was never my forte, but I know my housecleaning habits are seriously lacking. I do know that having a sink full of dirty dishes doesn't make you a terrible mother. When the kids were little, there was so much going on, that cleaning took a back seat most days.

When people get older and closer to the end of their time on earth, you ask what regrets they have. They do not say I wish I had a cleaner house or I wish I had more time to clean that pesky ring around the bathtub. They usually say things like they wish they would have gotten more cuddles when their kids were little. They wish they would have danced more . . . things like that.

When Jonathan needs a hug, I will give him a hug. His security is knowing that I will lay and read if he wants to. We sit on the couch like bookends with our computers. He reaches over to hold my hand from time to time. That's how I want to be remembered . . . not with my head in the toilet or chasing around dust bunnies.

6. Don't say, "God only gives you what you can handle." It's not a horrible thing to say, but I get tired of hearing it. Some days, I felt I was in way over my head and not handling anything. In the beginning, I would ask God, "Why? Why me? I am not good at this. I am not doing a very good job with all of this." Someone told me that I must be special that God chose me to parent a special needs child. Thank you, God. I now realize how blessed I am.

September 13, 1998
   You smile, you coo, and you capture hearts. You are an adorable little boy who is anything but abnormal. We will wait patiently for you to walk, talk, etc. and with confidence knowing that you will have a wonderful life.
   You are a gift from God and life will be good for you. God bless you forever!

October 1998
Eve,

Jonathan is advancing so much faster than I expected. He could roll even with the casts. On his belly, he will lift his head and it brings tears to see him attempting to crawl. He will be crawling soon, walking soon after that and so soon he will be running with Raya.

10: IT TAKES A VILLAGE

The saying that it takes a village to raise a child is so true. We have wonderful friends who were and still are the best. What I am today (somewhat sane) and my children, I owe to my thoughtful and caring friends.

Jonathan was born with club feet. They looked like little frog legs. The orthopedic surgeon started seeing him right away in the NICU. As soon as he was home from the hospital, we had to go to their office and had casts put on his little legs. We had to go back every week and get new casts.

Jonathan's legs in casts.

The hard part was that we had to take off the casts ourselves. The night before his appointment, we would work on them. It was not an easy process. It took at least two people at least two hours. We placed him in an infant bathtub with lukewarm water and would try to soak them and we had a little saw we would use because the water would get cold, and we had to change it a lot. Jonathan was so patient but that would run out eventually. We had such good friends that would come and play with the girls and take turns holding Jonathan in the water while we worked on his casts.

It sounds terrible . . . big leg casts on such a little fella and, believe me, it looked terrible at first, but he used them to his advantage. He could use them to help himself roll over. I know his legs were stronger because of lifting those heavy casts all the time. He was such a trooper.

After the casts, he graduated to leg braces. These were tiny white shoes with steel braces on both sides of his legs connected to a band right below his knee. These were much more comfortable but we had to be careful they didn't dig into his skin. When he was laying down, he would tap his legs together, and the steel braces would make a clicking sound. He was very quiet, but he could really make some noise with leg braces.

July 9, 1998
   Babies grow so quickly that sometimes we miss the little accomplishments they make. With Jonathan, I know we will notice and cherish each step forward. We will appreciate each tiny sign that he gives us and will truly celebrate his signs of change.

The doctor wanted me to massage his feet morning and night. I was supposed to massage them and knead the muscles to the position they were supposed to be. He loved it.

Even after his feet were "fixed' and in the proper position, he would plop his feet into my lap whenever he could. We would be sitting on the couch reading or watching a movie and, plop, I had little feet in my lap! He did that for many years.

We have met so many wonderful, caring people through Jonathan. His teachers, aides, and therapists who were so dedicated to his well-being.

June 2, 1998

I know that life with a child with Down syndrome will not always be easy for your parents. But as a mother I know life with any child can be difficult and each of our lives is never free of heartache and pain. So, I continue to remind myself that the extra work in raising you will bring extra joy for each person fortunate enough to know and love you.

Jonathan, you are unique, a marvel in your own way. You are a joy at times and a terror sometimes. You possess a little extra genetic material which will influence your growth and development, which while making you different will prove to make you special. You may not learn in the same way, or even in the same order as other children but you will learn. That extra chromosome has worked its spell on your facial features but you are adorable and capture the hearts of those who have been fortunate enough to receive a peek at you. You squiggle and wiggle like all infants. Your cry sounds like all infants. Your cry sounds like a kitten's meow. You are difficult to wake for feedings but when awake, try to soak in everyone and everything around you.

Each child, each person is different . . . a unique individual put on this earth to offer something to those around us. Your life is a gift to us.

I am usually pretty good about handling situations. I don't get hysterical when things go wrong. I get stressed and then move on to the next thing. I sweep things under the rug until I can deal with them later. Well, sometimes later never comes and the things under the rug pile up. They build until it blows up in my face. On one occasion I was having trouble dealing with life's difficulties. I knew I had to get away or I would lose my mind. I threw the kids in the car. I don't even remember packing their clothes. I drove an hour and a half to my friend's place. They have a cabin that I can use for a retreat for myself. My two friends took the kids for two days to give me a little break. It really helped me clear my head. I just sat and cried and read and cried and slept. I don't know what I would have done without my friends. I still don't know what I would do without them.

11. SPEECH THERAPY

I decided this needed a chapter all by itself. Jonathan had a lot of therapy . . . physical, occupational, behavioral, and speech. He graduated from everything but speech therapy. His biggest delay has always been speech and language. His receptive speech (hearing and comprehending what is being said) is fine. He is just so hard to understand. When you are around him long enough, it's easier to understand what he is saying. It is very frustrating for him and me.

The speech therapist started coming to the house soon after he was home from the hospital. She worked on his sucking reflex and strengthening his facial and oral muscles. She came once a week. These services were through early intervention. Early intervention has services for babies to age three. At age three through school age, the children have services through the intermediate unit.

Jonathan sucked his tongue. One day, when the speech therapist came for a visit, he was sitting in his high chair. It was only the second or third time that she saw him. She said, "Still sucking his tongue, I see." I was crushed and didn't know what to say. I wasn't sure if that was something I was supposed to be working on with him or if it was a bad thing. I don't think she meant anything bad was happening, but as a new mother, I was very self-conscious of everything Jonathan did and needed to be doing.

He still sucks his tongue, especially when he is tired. I got used to it. Jonathan is Jonathan, whether he sucks his tongue or not. It is a source of comfort for him.

Over the years, we have had many different speech therapists. I know I have had lofty and possibly unrealistic expectations for the speech therapists. I wanted results, and I wanted improvement, and I wanted it immediately! I know I should have worked with him more and I had good intentions, but life was always so busy. The girls had sports activities and homework. There was dinner to be made and cleaning to do. The grass needed to be mowed and hedges begged to be clipped. Life was just so crazy.

One speech therapist that Jonathan had in elementary school wasn't licensed. She was working with an emergency certificate. That was legal if she was taking classes in speech pathology. She had no experience. It was appalling. She spent most of the speech sessions trying to get Jonathan to sit still instead of working with his busy body. She did recommend that we see a private speech therapist in the summer months. I was grateful for this. It was a huge help for Jonathan's speech.

We drove an hour one way to see this recommended therapist. We went every other week all summer long. I tried to incorporate activities along with this trip. The girls would go along sometimes and we would go to a museum or shopping. I was glad when they went along so they could see what he was working on and how to work with him. They were very helpful in practicing his sounds and words.

I used to go in the room with him when the speech therapist took him back. I could see what they were working on. One time, I fell asleep. My head in my arms, on the little table! How embarrassing! Raya had me up the night before with a toothache, and I just couldn't keep my eyes open any longer! She didn't ask me back in the room with them anymore. I probably snored! She let me stay in the waiting room from then on.

We had a speech therapist in middle school that I just didn't click with. It's hard to work with someone that you just don't respect. Like I said, I was a little critical of his speech therapists. She finally told me that his speech was what it was. With his lack of articulation, it wasn't going to get any better. This infuriated me. It motivated me to get more involved in his therapy. I took him to our summer speech therapist all year long for as long as our insurance would allow. Our 'summer' therapist said, "There isn't a sound he can't make. He just needs practice and motivation."

Since Jonathan and I seem to spend so much time on the road, I try to take advantage of him being a captive audience. He usually has his iPad. He has a language program called Proloquo. It was an expensive program that I bought but has been worth every penny. His teacher is wonderful about adding words and items that pertain to his everyday living. She puts his spelling words on there also.

When I don't know what he is saying, I ask him to show me on his iPad.

He loves to go through all the words and make me say them with him. I try to add words together to form small sentences. He says, "Mom, road."

I say, "What about the road? Do I like the road? Do I drive on the road?"

He looks around on his iPad for a little. Then says, "Mom throw road." This is good. We are forming sentences. Then he says, "Mom throws poop road." He has a huge gut busting laugh about this, but he has formed a four-word sentence. This is one of those times, that I am not sure what is appropriate as a mother. I am so grateful for his sentence building skills, but I am not sure of the content. If his silliness helps him make sentences and build his "language (not always appropriate)" skills, I am okay with it for now. I made a mental note to ask his teacher about this. I made a mental note to make a real note about this. My mental notes don't last very long!

12. DOCTORS

We have been to so many doctors and specialists and I feel that Jonathan is healthy. I feel so bad for kids that have more issues than Jonathan has. In the beginning, I think I panicked a lot, always expecting the worse. His pediatrician never made me feel bad, though. In fact, I feel we had a pretty good doctor for a pathetic mother of a special needs child, relationship. I feel she trusted my instincts and valued my opinion. We have been through a lot together!

I am the mother who interviews the pediatrician before making an appointment. When Miranda was small, a new pediatrician moved to the area. I set up an interview and she passed the test! She was the mother of three small children and was very professional. These are some points that are very important to me. I knew it was the right place for us when Miranda ran from the exam room in only underwear. She made a lap around the back area before I corralled her back to the exam room. No one got upset or made comments. The new pediatrician's office was a hit!

When Jonathan was born, she assured me that she had experience with children with Down syndrome and felt comfortable with his needs. She even gave me her home number in case I would need her after hours. She only worked part-time. I really, really appreciated this. It was like a lifeline being thrown to me because I was scared to death.

Our pediatrician got more than she bargained for. When Raya first came from China, she had many potential health concerns to rule out. Our first appointment with her was also a checkup for Jonathan. We were there for two hours! She was with us for a full two hours! Some things we could do at the same place and same time. This saved some time but was very crazy. Those were the crazy days.

Some specialists we have been to (and I think I have forgotten some):
Pediatric Ophthalmologist
ENT
Pediatric Dermatologist
Pediatric Cardiologist
Pediatric Gastroenterologist
Orthopedic surgeons
Orthotic specialists

When Jonathan was around one year old, he developed a weird rash on his face and neck. It looked like red, pinpointed round spots (petechiae). I was petrified because I looked it up and found out that it could be the result of bleeding or leukemia which kids with Down syndrome are more prone to acquire.

In a panic, I called the doctor and hoped she wouldn't think I was overreacting. She got us right in for an appointment. I could tell that she was concerned, but did not know what it was. She sent us to a Pediatric Dermatologist at a facility one and a half hours from home. My girlfriend, Pam, met us there. She was a pharmaceutical salesperson and was in the area. I was so grateful for her company. I always got so worked up about potential issues, I didn't always

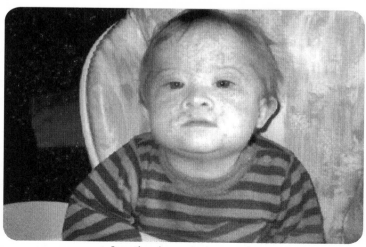

Jonathan's mysterious rash.

ask the right questions or I would forget things the doctor would say. It was good to have another ear.

The doctor spent a lot of time with us and took blood tests (poor Jonathan was always having blood drawn). He ruled out anything serious and thought it was a viral infection. What a relief! Our prayers were answered again.

We went back to the Pediatric Dermatologist about a year later for Jonathan's constant diaper rash. His skin was so sensitive. The doctor thought that he should not be wearing cloth diapers at all. He wanted Jonathan to wear only disposable diapers. I hated to use disposable diapers 100% of the time, because of their negative impact on the environment and because of cost. But, that was the end of my noble causes diaper-wise. Disposable diapers really did help his skin. That cute doctor was right again!

Eye disease is reported in over half the people with Down syndrome. This could be from a range of things from tear duct abnormalities to early-age cataracts. Because of the upward slanting of the eyelids, there are prominent folds of skin between the eye and nose. Also, small white spots on the iris are common. These spots are harmless and can also be found on people without Down syndrome.

The need for corrective lenses (eyeglasses) is much more common for people with Down syndrome than for the general population. This can be because of farsightedness, astigmatism, or nearsightedness. Another problem can be weak muscle tone or difficulty changing focusing power of the eye from seeing things at a distance to seeing them closer. Another problem is eye misalignment. Jonathan doesn't need glasses, but he gets his eyes examined every three years. Also, tear duct abnormalities are common. Jonathan did have problems with his tear ducts. We put warm compresses on his eyes and used eye drops.

Up to 80% of children with Down syndrome have hearing loss ranging from mild to severe. This could be caused from chronic ear infections, anatomical differences (typically smaller ear canals), and weaker immune systems. Jonathan's ears are tiny. His ear canals are tiny. Whenever a physician looks, they always must get a smaller scope. The eustachian tubes are typically smaller and anatomically more horizontal than "normal" in people with Down syndrome. This makes it harder for fluid to drain.

Hearing is so vital for speech and language development. Even mild hearing loss can make it more difficult to learn new words, delaying clear speech. Simply having fluid in the eustachian tubes with no actual hearing loss makes it difficult to hear. Having fluid in one's eustachian tubes is like trying to hear while being underwater. Imagine trying to comprehend what someone is saying underwater, then trying to replicate that sound. It makes a hard situation even harder.

We found a great ENT (Ears, Nose, and Throat specialist). His name is Dr. S and he loved Jonathan and still does. He placed tubes in his ears to help fluid drain. Things were great for a while. His tubes came out on their own, which is normal, the doctor assured me several times. Jonathan's eustachian tubes looked improved. He was cleared from going to see Dr. S.

When Jonathan was nine, he had a lot of colds, sinus infections, and nasal congestion. He was constantly being treated for something. I talked to the pediatrician about it and she agreed we should pursue it. So, back to Dr. S we went. Jonathan had scans and tests run. The prognosis was to have his tonsils and adenoids removed. I was not surprised by this. He also had polyps in his sinus cavity. This was a surprise. We scheduled surgery at a local hospital in August 2007.

I was a wreck. Neither one of us could eat that morning. He couldn't have anything because of pre-op instructions and I couldn't get anything in my churning stomach.

We met with Dr. S and the anesthesiologists before the surgery. The pre-op nurses got him in his little gown and already on the gurney to be wheeled back to the operating room. We were waiting in the hallway for the room to be ready and Dr. S walked by on his way to the surgery. He stopped for last-minute comments. Dr. S always teased me about being such a worrywart.

Jonathan lifted his arms to Dr. S. Dr. S picked him up and carried him into surgery. The Dr. looked back over his shoulder at me and said, "How am I supposed to do surgery on him now?"

The surgery that was supposed to take 45 minutes instead took one and a half hours. I was beside myself. Dr. S came out to tell me that everything went well. They removed his tonsils, adenoids, polyps in the sinus cavity, and did some reconstruction in the sinus as well.

Then a nurse called me back to the recovery room. He was having a tough time coming out of anesthesia. They usually don't call parents back so soon, but thought I might be helpful getting him to come around. He had been thrashing around and somewhat combative. I tried to calm him but was having trouble myself.

He was finally settled enough to move from post-op to a private room. They wanted us to stay overnight with an oxygen mask on. I laid in bed with him to try to keep the mask in place. He kept moving and was very restless. It was hard to keep the mask in place.

The next morning, I discovered that Jonathan had been given too much morphine. Three different sources told me. We got our post-op instructions and got discharged. I was never so glad to be going home.

When I called the hospital to speak to someone in quality assurance, I couldn't get any definitive answers. I wanted to tell them how horrible the anesthesiology team was. I wanted a follow-up or an apology, but I didn't get anything and I didn't have the energy to pursue it. The surgery was successful for Jonathan. He didn't have any major issues for several years. Jonathan's reconstructed sinuses and tonsil-less throat were doing great! He only got one or two colds per year. I was so pleased. We were members of a healthy household!

Just recently, I noticed that Jonathan kept saying "huh" and "what" a lot. I really noticed when we were in the car. I thought it was a teenager thing, he was using his selective hearing. I asked his doctor, and she recommended I see Dr. S again to check it out. I also wanted to check his oral cavity to make sure there wasn't anything anatomically out of order. I wanted to make sure everything possible was being done for his speech. I also wanted to ask about sleep apnea. I didn't think Jonathan was sleeping very well. I was reading some research that indicated if he sits in a curled-up position during sleep, it's a good indication that he has sleep apnea.

His mouth checked out with no abnormalities there. Dr. S. gave us some nasal spray to help him sleep because he was stuffy. He said you do not want Jonathan to have sleep apnea. I don't think he would like to wear a C-pap machine. "No, he would not," I thought.

They performed a hearing test. Lo and behold, he had hearing loss in his left ear-the ear that faces me in the car. I was flabbergasted. I thought maybe the cause was some wax build-up or something that could be easily remedied. Wow.

The next step was to make an appointment with an audiologist. I wanted to go to one that was highly recommended. I didn't think that insurance would pay all of it, but that's ok. I also needed to call and check with the insurance company to see if they will cover another hearing test. The audiologist needed to do their own test.

We made the appointment and I liked the audiologist. She saw lots of kids and Jonathan's goofiness made her laugh. They performed the hearing test and it wasn't easy because of his lack of speech clarity. The doctor had an intern go in the room with him and help. They used pictures.

His hearing loss turned out to be worse than we thought. He had nerve damage. The audiologist said it could have been like that for quite some time. Boy, did I feel like the mother of the year. He had hearing tests at school, but they weren't as detailed as professional hearing tests. Jonathan must have overcompensated with the good ear! The good ear had some hearing loss also, but not significant.

The audiologist took a mold of his ear and Jonathan got to pick out colors for his brand-new hearing aid. He chose green (my favorite color) for the outside part, and blue and yellow (his favorite colors) for the part that goes in his ear.

A week later, we went in to get the hearing aid. He was not a fan! The audiologist adjusted it using the computer. He kept saying, "loud." It was so very different for him. She had to be careful because of his tiny ear canals, so more adjustments were made. We left with batteries, cleaners, and instructions on the care of this tiny piece of expensive equipment. He was very disgusted. I was still feeling sorry for myself that I didn't pick up on his hearing loss sooner. Maybe, his speech could have improved earlier. The audiologist said usually it only affects speech when hearing loss is at a young age, and he only had a loss in one ear which made me feel a little better. I am hopeful though, for some improvement in speech when he can hear adequately out of both ears!

I decided we both needed a distraction. We met Clay and Miranda for dinner. That always makes him feel better. Miranda fusses over him and Clay likes to tease him. We were sitting in the restaurant and the ice dropped in the ice making machine. This is a sound we don't even think about normally . . . just an everyday sound in the restaurant world. Jonathan jumped when he heard it. It was either very loud to him or he was not used to hearing it!

When we went home and got ready for bed, I removed the hearing aid very carefully. He said "Whew". This poor little guy goes through so much but adapts so well. By the next day or two, he was already okay with it. He even reminded me to take it out before his bath!

For a while, he would joke about it. Miranda asked if he could hear better with it and he put his hand up to his ear and said, "Huh? What did you say?" He always liked to get a laugh!

Jonathan's Various Appointments
OCTOBER 2016 – AUGUST 2017

DATE	ISSUE

2016

October. . . . . . . Noticeable pain off and on
October 10 . . . . Routine medicine check up with Pediatrician
October 27 . . . . Meeting with our supports coordinator
November 10 . . Appointment with Dr. K - initial mention of hearing loss
November 10 . . Appointment with dentist - small cavity filled
November 10 . . Parent/Teacher conference
December 2 . . . Neurologist appointment (1 ½ hours away)
December 8 . . . Appointment at Orthodontist
December 9 . . . Consult with Physician Assistant of Neurosurgeon #1
December 16 . . Appointment with Cardiologist - annual check-up

2017

January 19. . . . Physical with Pediatrician
January 19. . . . Appointment with Orthodontist
February 2 . . . . Appointment with Dr. S - ENT
February 3 . . . . Meeting with supports coordinator
February 15 . . . MRI with sedation
February 16 . . . Consult with Neurosurgeon #1 - fitted for soft neck brace
February 16 . . . Appointment with Gastroenterologist - annual check-up
March 2 . . . . . . Appointment with Dr. L - audiologist - get hearing aid
March 3 . . . . . . IEP meeting
March 16 . . . . . Meeting with supports coordinator
March 24 . . . . . Appointment with Dr. L - check
March 30 . . . . . Appointment at Orthodontist
April 13 . . . . . . Evaluation with Neurosurgeon #1
April 26 . . . . . . Teacher called, Jon in extreme pain
April 27 . . . . . . Appointment with Dr. K
April 27 . . . . . . Appointment at Orthodontist - braces removed - YAY!
May 4 . . . . Cervical x-rays and evaluation with Neurosurgeon #1
May 4 . . . . Appointment at Orthodontist - retainers
June 8 . . . . Appointment at Pediatrician - med check
June 9 . . . . Consultation with Neurosurgeon #2 - fitted for hard neck brace
June 22 . . . . . . Appointment at Orthodontist
July 3. . . . . Consult with Neurologist
July 13. . . . . . . Appointment with Dr. L - hearing aid not fitting right
July 21. . . . . . . Appointment with Dr L - sore in ear from hearing aid
July 28. . . . . . . Consult with Neurosurgeon #3--GREAT NEWS!!!!
August 4. . . . . . Appointment with Dr. L - molds for new hearing aid
August 18. . . . . Meeting with supports coordinator
August 31. . . . . Appointment with Dr. L - new hearing aid

13. NECK PROBLEMS

Atlantoaxial Instability (AAI) is another health issue that kids with Down syndrome are prone to develop. Jonathan had a cervical x-ray when he was three years old. Everything checked out with no signs of AAI. Silly me, thought that was it, never to be worried about again. Once more, I was proven wrong. Once more, I felt like the mother of the year.

AAI is excessive movement in the junction between the first and cervical vertebrae (C1 and C2). It is the result of a bony or ligamentous abnormality. Neurological symptoms can occur when the spinal cord is involved.

The pressure on the spinal cord can produce symptoms such as pain, numbness, and tingling in the arms and legs. Early signs can be a change in behavior, refusal to participate in usual activities, changing hand preference, and urinary incontinence. More signs are dizziness, vertigo, ringing in the ear, fainting, and a change in gait (walk).

In October 2016, Jonathan complained of neck pain off and on . . . mostly in the tub. I think when he was arching his head back to wash his hair. He started to complain about other times too. I didn't think much of it, because he is so active. I wrote it on my list to ask Dr. K about on our next visit.

His next visit for a checkup coincidentally happened to be the end of November. She was concerned enough to send us for an x-ray. Lo and behold . . . he had instability in his first and second vertebrae. Dr. K. wanted us to go to a neurosurgeon to be checked.

We had our annual appointment with our neurologist soon after that appointment. I never knew that a neurologist and neurosurgeon were two different things! I am learning so much as I go.

A neurologist is a specialist that diagnoses and treats disorders that affect the brain cord and nerves, central nervous system disorders like Multiple Sclerosis, stroke, and seizure disorders.

A neurosurgeon specializes in the diagnosis and surgical treatment of the nervous system . . . trauma, tumors, infections of the brain and spine, just to name a few. A neurosurgeon has longer schooling and a longer residency.

He was so reassuring and helpful. He told me what to ask the surgeon and not to be afraid to have a second opinion. He said it happens all the time in their field.

The next step was to meet with the neurosurgeon. Miranda took off work to go with me. We thought they might want to take an MRI that day. We were so wrong. We had regular cervical x-rays taken and met with the physician's assistant. She was very nice, but we were disappointed that we went to all the trouble to rearrange our schedules and didn't even talk to the surgeon.

We scheduled an appointment for a cervical MRI. This took a couple of months before it occurred because he had to be sedated for it. Again, Miranda and I took off work. We were going to try without sedation first but decided just to go with the sedation. It went very well.

Then, we made an appointment with the neurosurgeon to discuss the results. I wished I would have had someone along, but I couldn't ask Miranda to take off work again. I know neurosurgeons have many years of schooling and are so bright, but he was a pediatric neurosurgeon, so I thought he would have a little more personality. I got so overwhelmed with what he said and I even wrote things down.

He wanted Jonathan to wear a cervical neck brace for six weeks to see the results. If Jonathan felt better with the collar, that would be an indication that surgery would be beneficial. This would show that his neck benefited from the stabilization provided by the collar.

We got fitted for the collar and he adapted very well. He was a trooper. I think he enjoys the attention he gets! I just couldn't wrap my head around the reasons for surgery and what the surgeon said. I sent him an email and he called me. He was very accommodating in answering my questions. I think he "dumbed it down" for me! I think I just have a mental block when it comes to talking about cervical spine surgery.

When we went back for the follow-up appointment, I took my boyfriend along. I felt that the doctor treated me with more respect and was more patient. I was nervous. Jonathan did well with the collar. I thought that was an indication that surgery was needed. The surgeon said Jonathan was clear to do all activities and wear the collar just as needed. This was not what I expected, but I was glad for the results.

Without the collar, Jonathan suffered from severe neck pain. He had headaches and loss of cognition at school. He sat in the tub holding his chin. He asked to wear the neck collar. I called the pediatrician and got him in to see her right away. She wanted me to go back to see the neurosurgeon, and the neurologist to possibly have an MRI on his brain. We decided that I would feel better with a second opinion from a neurosurgeon at a different facility.

I made the second opinion appointment at a medical facility that is one and a half hours away. This distance was not a big deal. We have been there before for other appointments. I took my mother along. She and Jonathan took turns riding shotgun! He sat up front on the way and she sat up front on the way back. I was feeling very confident. I had my paperwork done. I had Jonathan's x-rays on discs. I was even feeling a little cocky. I was proud to show off my "appointment going" skills to my mother. I had my notebook with all the pertinent questions I should ask. I had come so far from that "Nervous Nelly "of 19 years ago when Jonathan was first born.

Mom waited for us in the waiting room. Jonathan and I went in. I liked the neurosurgeon immediately. I felt comfortable. He recommended surgery for Jonathan, without a doubt. He felt his range of motion was impaired and not having surgery could be detrimental to Jonathan's well-being. The surgery doesn't come without side effects though. We discussed all the pros and cons, risks and benefits. He said we could wait until Jonathan had more pain, numbness, etc., but that wasn't what he recommended.

My confident stride going into the consultation was replaced by a slow, uncertain walk going out. My head was reeling. I had so much to think about. I barely spoke on the way home. I gave myself a headache thinking about it so much.

My mother felt so bad that she gave me the end table, in her living room, that I had been wanting. She called me the next day to say that she was glad she went along and that Jonathan is such a pleasure to be with. She told me to pray to find an answer. I was beside myself. I had two very different opinions. I had many sleepless nights. I felt like my head was going to explode at times. My stomach churned when I would think about Jonathan having this invasive surgery. He would have to wear a "halo" head restriction and be out of commission for a couple of months. That would be pure torture for him. There are many complications with surgery, some being fatal.

I asked many people with medical expertise, what their opinion was. What would they do if they were me? I even talked to Jonathan's orthodontist, Dr. B, about it. His brother-in-law is a neurosurgeon in Kentucky. I would have gone to Kentucky if I had felt it would be beneficial. Dr. B asked his brother-in-law where we should go. We decided on the Children's Hospital of Philadelphia.

I called and made the appointment. I had to go to the first Neurosurgeon and get a copy of the x-rays and MRI. It was not a hard process, just time consuming (like everything). I didn't want to go to the appointment alone. I was starting to get concerned. Then I asked our family friend, Diane. She's my sister's best friend and I have known her forever. She was glad to go along.

I was so sure that the neurosurgeon would say that he would need surgery. I was planning. I was saving my vacation time at work. I felt that whatever this neurosurgeon said was the best recommendation for Jonathan, we would do. We would have the surgery there. The hospital was over two hours away. I would take off work and stay with Jonathan. The recuperation would take time.

We decided to take the train. It would be a two-hour ride and we wouldn't have to worry about traffic. Diane's husband took us to the train station, so I didn't have to worry about parking and paying for it. It was great to be dropped off at the train station door with no worries.

I was worried enough about the appointment. I had done a lot of research and had two pages of notes and questions to ask. Diane had also done some research and brought her notes and was ready to write things down. We sat comfortably on the train and compared our notes. Jonathan brought his iPad, so he was content. We had a pleasant trip.

We had to take a short taxi ride to the hospital. The hospital was huge, very overwhelming. We checked in and had to get badges to wear. We found out where we were supposed to go and Jonathan got to ride an elevator. His favorite part of the trip! Everyone was very nice to us. It was very humbling to walk around a children's hospital. It put things into perspective for me.

We didn't have to wait long and were taken back to an operatory. We sat there listening to our surroundings (I am a little nosy)! We heard the doctor come and go rather quickly with other patients. Diane and I were worried that he would be quick with us and all our concerns. We saw him in the hallway and Diane said, "Well, he's a long, tall drink of water!" He was tall and gorgeous!

When it was our turn, he walked into the operatory and we were in awe. He was so nice and when we picked our jaws up off the floor and gathered our wits, it went very well. He was so patient and explained so well. I wasn't intimidated at all. He showed me Jonathan's x-rays and made sure we knew exactly what he was talking about. He spent a lot of time with us and I didn't feel rushed at all.

The best news was that Dr. Cutie Pie didn't feel that Jonathan needed surgery. I couldn't believe it. I kept asking him if he was sure! He stated that the criteria have changed and that they don't like to do surgery so readily anymore. I asked him if Jonathan would have to be careful and not do the things that he enjoyed. I didn't want him to be playing basketball and must worry that something catastrophic would happen. The doctor assured me that Jonathan would be fine, his neck would not break. Jonathan is to stay away from high contact sports, like football, etc.

The doctor wanted to see a cervical x-ray in six months to see if there were changes. He said we could have the x-ray taken closer to home and sent to him. Diane and I said, "We don't mind coming down to CHOP. It's no trouble at all!" He replied, "Unless, he's having problems, I don't need to see Jonathan, just monitor him through x-rays."

When we left the operatory, I was walking on air. When we were outside of the hospital and waiting for a cab, Jonathan and I did a happy dance. I felt like a weight had been lifted off my shoulders. We were all so relieved.

14. OUR GUARDIAN ANGEL

My children were fortunate to have a very special aunt in their lives, if only for a short time. It was, in fact, way too short. She was taken from us when she was only forty years old. She lived in Michigan, but still managed to be an important part of our lives.

She had a smile that lit up the room and a laugh that was contagious. I feel honored to have been her sister-in-law/friend for such a short time. Anyone who knew her loved her. She was kind of short, but what she lacked in height, she made up for in personality! She had long dark hair and beautiful eyes. I remember her rushing

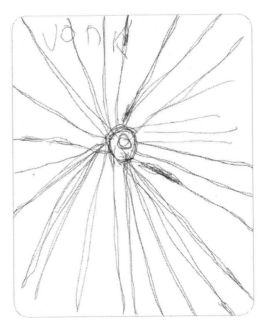

in the door at family events, her arms filled with bags. She always brought snacks (healthy or otherwise) and gifts for the kids.

When the kids were little, we decided to make a will and have a legal guardian for the kids. When we decided to ask Aunt D, I wasn't sure because of the distance. She lived eight hours away.

I spoke to her and told her of our decision. I wanted to know how she felt about this. I wanted to make sure she did not feel obligated or pressured in any way. I told her the decision was hers. We would totally understand either way. She was single and juggling both work and school.

She did not hesitate. She immediately said, "Of course, I will be the guardian. I will do whatever it takes. Isn't that what family does?"

The funny thing is that . . . Aunt D's other brother also asked her to be their guardian for their three children! She could have been a very busy aunt! She would have made it work, though. I am sure of it.

She's the one who sent cards, presents, and always had fun things for the kids to do. The kids were four, five, and ten when a motorcycle accident stole her from us. Our lives were changed forever.

For a long time, I had a huge, empty space in my heart. Sometimes, I would be driving and it would it hit me like a brick in my chest that she was gone. I couldn't breathe for a little bit. Her death seemed so unfair and horrific to me. I really struggled with this and doubted God's plan. How can someone so good be taken so quickly . . . so abruptly?

I contemplated my religious beliefs for some time. I was very angry at God. How could He take someone so good from our lives? How could we go on living normal lives without her being a part of it? We all had a really hard time dealing with her loss.

Then, I would have dreams about her. My dreams were so real, and she seemed so real. The dreams were about her and she was with us, doing things with us, but we were the only ones that could see her. I couldn't believe how she was with us again. I would wake up and realize it was only a dream. After several of these life-like dreams, I realized she was still with us and she would always be. She was our guardian angel. I believe God was telling me this through my dreams.

I am so thankful to have a guardian angel for the kids, especially, when I almost ran over Jonathan! I had a big old "Mom" van. I was slowly pulling into the driveway. It was not a very long driveway. The kids wanted out to play on the swing set. I left them out and continued slowly down the driveway . . . I repeat . . . slowly. I think it was Miranda who was yelling to stop. I stopped and got out of the van. Jonathan was pinned under the back tire by his jacket. He had a brand new bright yellow parka on. It was under the tire. My mind was racing. My adrenaline kicked in. I think I am usually pretty good under pressure. Thank goodness. I usually can handle the situation as it occurs, then have a meltdown afterward! I didn't know what to do. Miranda wasn't old enough to drive and she didn't want to hold him while I drove in reverse, just enough to get the tire off his jacket. She was scared, and I don't blame her. I was, too, and trying not to show it. I had her run in the house and get the scissors, while I held Jonathan, trying to keep him calm. Of course, the scissors were nowhere to be found (typical of our household). I told her to bring a knife and I would cut his jacket off. The knife wasn't very sharp, so it took a while, but we finally freed him of the tire. The ruined coat was a small price to pay for his being unscathed.

Afterward, I sat at the dining room table looking out the window at the scene of the "accident" and had a meltdown. I called my mom to come down (she only lived five minutes away), while I got calmed down. I put my head in my arms on the dining room table and cried. I contemplated on what could have happened and what didn't happen. We were very close to a disastrous ending. How horrible would that have been and all my fault? My mind was reeling. I knew our guardian angel was looking out for us. The good thing was, that I was restored in my faith again. Thank you, God and our Guardian Angel.

When this wonderful person left this earth, we went to her house to clear things out. We discovered a book, *The Joy of Signing*. She was taking it upon herself to learn sign language to communicate with Jonathan before we even planned on it. We had only mentioned it and she forged ahead because she wanted to be able to communicate with him. Miranda (who is a notorious book lover) quickly adopted the book and attempted to teach herself. Ten years later, when Miranda went to college, still possessing her earlier love for both sign language and her late aunt's book, she went on to minor in American Sign Language.

15. THINGS THAT KEEP ME AWAKE AT NIGHT

I am a huge worrier. I specialize in worrying about things that I have no control over. Makes total sense, right? I have always worried about whether I was doing the right thing regarding the kids. I guess most parents do. I feel like there should be a test you must take (and pass) to become a parent. My parents were good role models, but being the mother of a child with special needs was new to our family. We were in uncharted waters! Here are a few of the many things I worried about that would keep me awake at night . . .

1. I worried that there wasn't enough of me to go around. Miranda was an only child for five years. She was used to having all the attention. She prayed for a brother and sister, but it was a huge adjustment for her. Raya needed extra attention her first couple years of life to get caught up with developmental milestones. The first year of her life, she laid in a crib. She was fed but didn't have much stimulation, which is common for orphanages in China. She quickly caught up and surpassed all expectations. I prayed a lot that they were getting what they needed. And I prayed some more that they were getting the attention they needed. Now that it is just Jonathan and me at home. I feel I can devote more time to Jonathan and his activities.

2. I worried about Jonathan's breathing. I previously mentioned that Jonathan was sent home from the hospital without a heart monitor. The neonatologist didn't feel as if he needed it. They usually only send babies home with them if they have heart problems, not for babies with poor oxygen exchange. Well . . . I needed it! I wish there was something for parents, to make them sleep a little easier when having a newborn. Maybe I needed a heart monitor for myself!

In Jonathan's first two years of life, he had croup. Miranda and Raya never had croup, so I had no idea what I was dealing with. He would gasp for breath. It was such a struggle for him to get air into his little lungs. His tiny chest would suck in as he was struggling for air. The cough sounded like a seal barking. He was rushed by ambulance to the hospital one time until we could get it under control. He grew out of this, but it was very unsettling for those few years. And now . . .

3. I worry that Jonathan won't be able to read. We are a family of readers. We love books. He loves looking at books and magazines. His room is overflowing with books and magazines, but he can't read. I think I could be more aggressive with teaching him to read, but I hate to shove it down his throat. Usually, when the school day is over, he has had enough of academics. I am not giving up though.

4. I worry that he doesn't have friends. His teacher assured me that he gets along with everyone in his class. There is a boy that he hangs out with at school. He doesn't talk about anyone, though. I am used to having girls at my house and the craziness of Miranda and Raya's constant need for contact with friends.

We go to dances. There are two kids from his class there. He does not hang out with them though. He is very content to dance by himself. I sit and talk with the other mothers.

One time, when I was sitting there talking with the moms and watching him dance, the chicken dance started to play. I said to my friend, "Oh, he loves this dance." I got up and raced over to dance with him, thinking he would love it. He was humiliated. He told me to go, sit down! Maybe, I don't need to worry about him after all!

5. I worry about what he is going to do after graduation. There are group homes, but they are hard to get into. I am not sure what the best option for him is. When he was young, we always joked that he would be a doorman at a hotel because he was almost obsessive about opening doors for people. If someone else beat him to it, he took offense to it and would often hold the door so that they would release it. As part of his schooling, the teachers work with finding a task or occupation that is suitable for him. His class has affiliations with businesses in the community. The students get job coaches and perform the job duties at the business. After

Jonathan began his assignment at Giant, we quickly realized that he is a local celebrity there. Grocery trips morphed into a social hour with employees saying hi or high-fiving Jonathan. He loves to stock shelves in a store. I can also see him being a busboy in a restaurant. Jonathan was nine or ten when Miranda and I worked at a small local cafe. If it was slow when Jonathan came in, Miranda would let him bus and clean the tables. He loved it and we found that there weren't enough tables for him to clean. He is a hard worker.

6. I worry what I am going to do after he graduates. I don't know what I will do if he leaves home. Although, I realize it is healthy for him to be independent and not be with his mother forever. He is my baby, my buddy, my companion. He has grown into such a pleasure to be around. I can't imagine him living on his own. While I know that at some point, he will not be living with me, it's almost unimaginable. Many assume that the relationship is heavily weighted with his dependence on me but that couldn't be farther from the truth. I rely on him, his laughter, smiles, jokes, questions, and company as much as he relies on me for the mundane tasks of the day-to-day. As much as he likes to pretend that he wants out of the house, he tells Miranda that he misses me after a night or two of being away.

7. I worry that I am doing the right thing. As a mother, I always have and probably always will worry if I am doing the right thing. I am supposed to be making him more independent, but I do things for him that I should probably make him do himself (as my daughters remind me). I was especially self-conscious when Jonathan was misbehaved in public. I know people judged me with how I handled him and the situation. I don't know if I was doing the right thing. He would lie on the floor. I would try to pick him up. He had a way of escaping your grip when he was throwing a tantrum. We dubbed this move "spaghetti arms." If he was throwing a fit and you tried to pick him up to remove him from the situation, he would lift his arms above his head, and wiggle them in a way that allowed him to slip out of getting picked up.

Every. Single. Time.

He wasn't cooperative. It was so frustrating. I was humiliated on many occasions. I know that some people weren't always happy to see us as visitors in their homes. However, through a combination of loving discipline, repetition, and him maturing, we have reached a stage where he is typically better behaved than I am in public anymore! He has always loved to hold hands. It is soothing for him. It is an instinct for him to reach out and grab my hand. When is he too old to hold his mother's hand? Am I doing him a disservice by always holding his hand? His teaching staff discouraged some of his behaviors, hand holding included. It's difficult to tell your son that you can no longer hold his hand. We tried to find a happy medium and only hold hands at night when he needed some extra help to relax. We tried to explain some behaviors are only done at home, not school, hand holding is one of them. He nodded his head and agreed but differentiating when behaviors are acceptable and when they are not is hard, especially for him. How hard should I push him toward more independence? Sometimes, it is just easier for me to do things for him. I don't always have the time or patience to let him do things himself. He feels so good about learning how to use the microwave. It's instinct for me just to do it myself. I must slow down and get him to stand there and follow the prompts and pictures.

I struggle over how much independence to give him and what age-appropriate activities he should do. Miranda and I don't always agree when it comes to this. She feels that even though developmentally he is younger, he can still enjoy some activities that a typically developing 19-year-old male would enjoy. Jonathan went to a Phillies' baseball game with her and Clay. Before the game, they grabbed a bite to eat at a bar. Jonathan sat at the bar with them and ordered Sprite. He chatted with the bartender and cheered with the patrons. He left with a baseball mitt that the very sweet bartender had gifted him. One thing I've found is that when you go out with a child with Down syndrome, you'll always find friendly strangers who have had a neighbor, cousin, sister, etc., with Down syndrome. They typically go out of their way to say hi and give a smile and a story (or baseball mitt). It's a little community all in itself!

Feb. 27, 1999

So, don't be anxious about your tomorrow. God will take care of your tomorrow, too. Live one day at a time.

—Matthew 6:34

16. GRAMMY

Jonathan and his grandmother have a special bond. They adore each other. He calls her Me-Me. I think he tried to say Grammy, like his sisters, but it came out Me-Me and stuck for him. When Jonathan was first born, Mom had a hard time accepting his diagnosis. I think she was afraid of what the future had in store for us. We were all a little afraid of that scary future. We were afraid of how fragile he was. Then, she welcomed him with open arms, literally. Jonathan stayed small and cuddly a lot longer than other babies. He loved to cuddle with Grammy. She would just sit and hold him or read to him. He was very content and I could get some things done.

Mom would go on vacations and day trips with us. Mom and Jonathan have nicknames for each other in the car. She is Mim and he is Freckles (because he is covered with freckles). I am not sure how they came up with Mim. I think one day they were being goofy! Much to my chagrin, she also taught him a little jingle. It goes, "He has freckles on his butt, he is nice." Then, they sing, "The bear went over the mountain." My mother cannot, and I repeat cannot, carry a tune. They laugh hysterically at my discomfort! My next book may be about the adventures of Mim and Frecks.

They take turns sitting in the front seat. When Mom is in the front and Jonathan is in the back, he leans up to hold her hand or talk to her. Jonathan opens her car door for her and takes special care of his grandmother.

When we go on a trip, Mom always brings snacks-usually fruit. She brings a little paring knife, napkin, and container to put fruit in, to pass around. Jonathan expects her snacks and will eat anything she has for him. He doesn't always do that for me! We had

to ban Me-Me from taking her paring knife along on plane trips, since 9/11. It was a sad time for us all when she couldn't pare apples on a plane and get curious stares from strangers!

Mom always makes his favorite foods when he is at her house. She makes him split-pea soup, Jello and his all-time favorite, barbeque with cheese. He walks in her door and asks for cheese. I think she feeds him every three hours when he is there!

Mom would go along to some doctor appointments when I needed a hand. When the kids were small, it was tough to pay attention to the doctor with all the kids in the room with us. Mom would either go along and occupy a child or two or she would stay at home with a child. Mom absolutely refused to go along if they had to take blood. Jonathan had blood drawn at least two times a year. It usually took four or five people to hold him down. It was an awful experience.

They are both hard of hearing. When we are in the car, I must be the interpreter or just block them out! I wish we would have taught her sign language. I hear a lot of "huh" and "what" when they are together.

They also both shuffle their feet when they walk. When we go anywhere together, I let them walk together and I walk ahead of them. I can still hear the shuffle, shuffle of feet.

When we go grocery shopping together, Jonathan wants to be with Grammy. He either pushes his own cart and follows her or pushes her cart for her. Thank goodness for her patience, because I can buzz around the store like a bird when I don't have to worry about someone running into my ankles with a cart!

We stay overnight at Mom's about one or two nights a month. Jonathan has his own room there! I leave some extra clothes there in case we need them. She fusses at me if my stuff isn't out of sight, but she doesn't say a word about his extra pajamas and socks. She gets up and makes him breakfast, just the way he likes it! I am not complaining though. They bring me coffee in bed!

Jonathan had his bike at Grammy's for a long time. In the basket, he kept his helmet and an old pair of winter gloves that Grammy gave him. He took his obligation to put these on very seriously. He wore the gloves, it didn't matter what the weather was. I think he believes he must wear them because Grammy gave them to him to wear for bike rides. His hands got mighty sweaty sometimes. He rode his bike around and around her house. He stopped and knocked at the front door every so often. I told Mom that he doesn't want anything, he is just knocking for the heck of it. I don't answer it. Mom does. She doesn't care. She likes to try to catch him before he hops back on his bike and rides away! They both get a big kick out of this. Mom told me that only special people have children with Down syndrome. God chose us. Thank you, God.

17. FAITH

I don't consider myself super religious. I am not perfect by any means. I have not always attended church regularly. I have done things that I am not proud of. I don't know my Bible as well as I should, for as much time as I have spent in church and church-related activities. I want to learn, though and I want to grow. I feel that the power of prayer is huge and has gotten me through so much.

I grew up going to church and Sunday school. We went to Bible school and church camp. I had a good church upbringing and am thankful to my parents for that. When I was a teenager, I joined the church and went to youth group every week. As I got older, I would go to church, just because I knew it pleased my mother.

When I was college-age and in my twenties, I was quite a partier. My girlfriend and I often discussed that we felt our good church upbringing kept us from going too far astray from the right path. I think God was looking out for us! Then, when I got older, I went to church because I wanted to and enjoyed it. I got married in the church and wanted to raise my children the way I was raised about religion. I made sure I told my husband-to-be how important it was to me to take our future kids to church. I think I did a good job with that. We had so many good times with our church friends when the kids were little. It was tough getting three kids ready for church on Sunday mornings. Sometimes, I was exhausted until we got there, but it was worth it. I felt such a peaceful, secure feeling sitting in church.

Next, came my rough patch. For several years, I didn't attend church regularly. When I got divorced, I didn't have the faith or feel worthy to be in church. When Jonathan was little, he wouldn't sit still in church and he didn't want to stay in junior church or nursery. I wasn't sure what to do and couldn't find a good fit for us.

As Jonathan got older and matured, it was easier to go. We found a church that we all liked. It wasn't ideal for Jonathan, but it was okay. Raya got me interested in Sunday school and I really enjoyed it. They had nothing for Jonathan, though. He had to sit with me or Raya in our Sunday school class. That made for long mornings for him when we had church afterward.

We now attend a great church. It is great for Jonathan and me. Last Christmas Eve, we were not attending any church regularly. It's part of our family tradition to go to church on Christmas Eve, so I found a church that had a time that worked for us. We all went . . . Grammy, Miranda, Clay, Raya, Jonathan, and me. Everyone was so friendly and welcoming, it felt great. We sat down in the pew, and I told Mom that I found my church. I could tell right away that I found what I was looking for.

Once a month, on a Sunday afternoon, the church has a special service for the all the churchgoers with special needs. They contribute to the service. They have hand instruments and stand up front to sing. It took Jonathan a couple of times to warm up, but now, look out! We sign (or say) the sharing of the peace. Then they have snacks afterward. The adults/caregivers can sit and socialize. We love it.

Jonathan wanted to join the children's choir at church. This was for fifth and sixth graders. This age group is a good fit for him. He goes to junior church with this age group. I just must make sure he is clean-shaven. He would stick out like a sore thumb with a full beard in this age group! I was so excited for him to be part of the church choir. I thought this would be great for Jonathan and a good way to get Miranda and Clay to come to church. My whole family and some family friends want to come to watch him sing.

I was so excited, but the first night of practice, I was a nervous wreck. There were five girls and two boys (including Jonathan). He wanted me to sit beside him. I was doubting my enthusiastic decision. I kept thinking, "was I doing this more for me or for him?" I was starting to think that maybe I made a mistake. Maybe, we should have stayed home, where we are comfortable. We were out of our comfort zone.

I thought the leader was a little nervous because she didn't know what to expect from Jonathan. She played a little game with cups, using a repetitive movement. He did well after a few tries. He does well with repetition.

Then she was teaching them a song that was written on the board. He can't read, but I would sing it, and he started to get the hang of it. He usually gets the last word of a stanza and it's about a word behind the rest of the kids.

Then she played a little game at the end, and everyone was so good about including Jonathan. I was so worried. I was concerned that the leader would want him to have a perfect performance. I asked the choir leader if he did okay. She said, "yes. he did great." She is so very patient. I asked her if it was okay if he just learned the chorus, and if it was a little slower. She said, "that would just add to it." Whew. I didn't realize how worried I was. On the way home, I felt like I could breathe again.

Jonathan's first performance in the children's choir at church was a success. I was worried that he would be silly, so I threatened him with Bert and Ernie. He wouldn't be able to watch them when we got home if he was silly during choir time! He didn't sing most of the words or very loudly, but he did whatever the leader was doing. She conducted the choir with her arms and so did he! Miranda asked me later if I got pictures. I said, "Are you kidding me? I was having trouble breathing!"

Once a year, my church has a Day of Pampering. This a special day of pampering for mothers of children with special needs. Approximately ninety women attend. There are women from the community too, not just our church. So of course, there is a waiting list, and not everyone can go every year.

A lot of planning and hard work goes into this special day and it is a grand production. So many people help with it. People donate their time, services, and more time. We are spoiled from the minute we walk in the door. It is an all-day affair from 9:00-4:00. We have a light breakfast, worship and reflection, special music, and blessing of the hands in the morning. The speaker is usually someone who has a child with special needs. The morning is usually very heartfelt and emotional.

Then we all go downstairs where the dining room is set up better than any fine dining establishment. Each table has a hostess who oversees her table, providing place settings and decorations. They are all beautiful. We are given a little bag filled with goodies and a full course meal for lunch.

The afternoon is filled with many services/luxuries that are at our fingertips. There must be eight hairstylists, several massage therapists and many others who donate their time to make sure that we have a day beyond our wildest dreams. Also available are hand waxing, nail polishing, eyebrow waxing, make-up application, reflexology, and healing touch.

We leave with our goodie bags, a bouquet of flowers, chocolates, and feeling like a queen. It's great to talk to other ladies in similar situations. I think the favorite part of my day is talking to the ladies at the dining table. Every year I seem to sit next to someone who has a small child with behavioral issues. My heart goes out to them. I love to be able to tell them that it does get better. I am proof. We have lived through it.

The first year, I sat beside a lady who had a son with Down syndrome. I believe she said he was five. She said she couldn't make him behave. He wouldn't listen to her. It reminded me of Jonathan at that age. I think I made her feel better by sharing some of our experiences and of Jonathan's current well-behaved manner.

A self portrait.

18. CLOSING

The writing of this part of our journey (I am looking forward to many more adventures) was therapeutic for me. It brought back many memories, and not all those memories were fond ones. I struggled with that, but I am proud to say I have moved forward, we all have. I feel that I can deal with life and its sometimes unpleasantness much better than I did previously. I am not sure how or why, but I feel more content. Maybe, I have just learned to expect the unexpected and go with the flow.

I recently heard a quote, "I am strong, but I am tired." That is exactly how I feel. My shoulders are strong enough to carry many burdens, but I get worn out at times. After a busy day of appointments and taking care of Jonathan things, I am tired. After, an IEP meeting, I am mentally exhausted.

When my weariness needs to be charged, I look to my faith, family, and friends. I pray daily to make the right decisions for Jonathan's well-being and future. I thank God daily for my strength, faith, family, and friends. My family and friends give me the encouragement I need to hear and an ear to listen to all our daily challenges. Just having someone listen is sometimes all I need.

I hope I managed to portray three points in my writing:

1.The importance of prayer. Pray, pray, pray, then pray some more. I truly do not know where we would be without prayer. God and our guardian angel are looking out for us. When I sit back and think of all the things that could have gone wrong in our lives, but didn't, I am grateful. Life was so hard at times, I wasn't sure how we would survive the storms. We weathered them and have become better people because of it. Thank you, God and Guardian Angel. It is reassuring to know that God is always in our presence. It might not seem like it or feel it at times, but around every corner, in every difficult situation . . . there is hope. Because we are not alone.

2. If I can do it, anyone can. If you are ever having doubts, I hope you will read this and think that if this crazy lady can raise three children unscathed (for the most part), you can too. I am not a mom who goes into meetings totally prepared or has all her ducks in a row. I am organized at being unorganized. I'm in control of managed chaos. Just keep plugging along. Life does get better, or maybe we get too worn out to care!

One time I had a meeting after work. My bedroom was in semi-darkness as I gathered my dress clothes to change into after work. Later, when I was changing, I realized I had two different shoes. That wouldn't have been too bad, but they were both left feet!

I repeat . . . if I can do this anyone can. Although, I am never too far from my bathrobe and slippers!

3. I owe Jonathan so much. He has taught us many things. His love for life and appreciation for everything are constant blessings. We have met so many wonderful people because of Jonathan. It has weeded out people that don't matter. If someone can't at least try to connect with Jonathan, they have no place in our lives. I have learned so much.

BELLE'S EMPLOYEE OF THE MONTH

Jonathan is not broken, he is exactly who he is supposed to be. Miranda and Clay got married September 3, 2016, at Belle Haven Farms. The owner, Tracy, really liked Jonathan. Whenever we would have a monthly meeting with her, she would have a snack for him. She converted her wedding business into a consignment shop and cafe. She approached us about utilizing Jonathan in her shop. She enjoyed his easy-going temperament and social skills. I believe the picture says it all!

Feb. 27, 1999
Your Jonathan is so wonderfully exceptional and you are the most fortunate to have received him. (Almost sounds like envy, doesn't it?) Every time I see him I am amazed that he is so perfect. His personality will outshine any handicap he may have. And his mother will be the fortunate one to have had the opportunity to be blessed with this gift.

42516855R00064

Made in the USA
Middletown, DE
20 April 2019